Dedication

This anthology was compiled principally ror the interest of my family and friends, for former colleagues and for former pupils. It is dedicated to all those who were members of that remarkable and distinguished English Department of The College of Richard Collyer in Horsham at various times during, or even throughout, the years when I was also there - from 1983 until 1999:

Gillian Anderton
Andrew Cairncross
Paul Clarke
Jenny Derbyshire
Kevin Halon
Anne Hinds
Sue Greenwood
Richard Jacobs
Penelope Maynard
Martin Nichols
David Sanderson
Phoebe Taplin
Jonathan Taylor
Paul Wakeling,
and also Ed Tattersall, Head of Classics, who
translated Latin and Greek for them as necessary.

They all knew far more about poetry than I do,
and it was a privilege to work with them.

Contents

		Page
Foreword		v
Acknowledgements		vii
The contents arranged alphabetically by authors		x

The anthology is arranged in ten sections, within each of which the poems are set out chronologically. The details of each section can be found on the pages indicated below:

		Page
I	15 Short Poems	2
II	15 Sonnets	8
III	15 Canticles and Psalms	18
IV	15 Poems on Aspects of Love	33
V	15 Poems about War and Peace	55
VI	15 Examples of Comic and Amusing Verse	73
VII	15 Narrative Poems	87
VIII	15 Hymns	131
IX	15 Longer Pieces	149
X	15 Favourites	183
Index of Opening Words		195

Foreword

My taste in music is what is often described as 'the popular classics': *Peer Gynt, The Siegfried Idyll* and *Finlandia*, for example, and above all *The Fantasia on a Theme by Thomas Tallis*. I treat music like wallpaper. It is pleasant to have music playing in the background while I am reading or writing, but I don't concentrate on it. Many people concentrate on music while it is playing to the exclusion of all else, and it is an important aspect of their lives. I don't, and it isn't.

But poetry is. I suppose the poetry I most like could also be described as 'the popular classics'. Much of it is well-known. All of it is readily accessible, and I have deliberately learnt by heart rather more than the one hundred and fifty pieces in this anthology. Although I spent my working life as a schoolmaster, poetry was not something I taught. Nor did I ever study it in the sense in which my colleagues who taught English Literature did. I taught History and left English Literature, including poetry, to others. I would have hated to try to teach teenagers about Keats's odes and find that they found them boring.

I learnt poems from an early age quite simply because I wanted to know them and wanted to be able to recite them to myself. No-one required me to do it. Soon I found that the process of learning them often led to understanding them better than I had beforehand. I also came to see how they were structured, and why some were easier and others more difficult to learn.

The longest poem in this anthology is from Longfellow's *Tales of a Wayside Inn*. It is *The Sicilian's Tale: King Robert of Sicily* (p.99). It can take nearly half an hour to recite it as I walk round Horsham Park, but it was relatively easy to learn for three reasons. First, it is in regular rhyming couplets of iambic pentameters. That is, it more or less follows the rhythm t'tum, t'tum, t'tum, t'tum, t'tum, and each couplet rhymes. Secondly, the sense of every phrase or sentence comes neatly to an end at the end of each line. In the whole poem there is only one instance of enjambement, which is where the sense runs over from one line to the next. That is where the angel says to King Robert:

> *"Nay, not the King, but the King's Jester, thou*
> *Henceforth shalt wear the bells and scalloped cape…*

The third thing which makes it relatively easy to learn is that it is a narrative poem divided conveniently into sections, each of which can be learnt separately.

A good example of a poem which is far more difficult to learn is Robert Browning's *My Last Duchess* (p.165). The difficulty lies in the fact that it is a continuous monologue with enjambement of most of the lines – nearly two-thirds of them, with ten or more lines at a time running the meaning over from one line to the next. It makes learning it difficult, but it is well worth the effort.

The way many poems are divided into sections helps with learning them. Sometimes the divisions are not immediately obvious. The twelve stanzas which comprise Keats's poem, *La Belle Dame Sans Merci* (p.42), divide conveniently into four groups of three. A poem which at first sight appears to be very irregular is Wilfred Owen's *Dulce Et Decorum Est* about a gas attack (p.66). It is set out in four sections, of eight, six, two and twelve lines. But it is composed in a standard ballad form, with seven stanzas, each with four lines of ten syllables and with a regular rhyme scheme: ABAB. The only deviation from this is in the last line, part of whose impact lies in the fact that it has only five syllables instead of ten.

I put this anthology together for friends and relations, former colleagues and former pupils, and I hope that some of them, and anyone else with a copy, may be encouraged to learn some of the poems. It's probably best to start with those which are both short and easy to learn. It can be very worthwhile.

David Arnold.   Horsham.   Summer 2021.

Acknowledgements

I would like to thank all those individuals and organisations who have given me permission to publish poems in copyright – about a third of those in this anthology. The other two-thirds are in the public domain.

Raffaella Barker, acting on behalf of her mother, Elspeth Barker, the Literary Executor for her late husband, Raffaella's father, George Barker, for permission to publish *To My Mother*.

Curtis Brown of New York for permission to publish *Funeral Blues*, also known as *IX of Twelve Songs*, and *Note on Intellectuals*, both by W. H. Auden. Copyright © W. H. Auden, renewed. Reprinted by permission of Curtis Brown, Ltd.

Faber and Faber Limited for permission to publish seven poems by Wendy Cope: *Two Cures for Love, Another Unfortunate Choice, Bloody Men, Flowers, After the Lunch, Valentine* and *My Funeral*; three items by T. S. Eliot: *Journey of the Magi, The Love Song of J. Alfred Prufrock*, and the soliloquy by Thomas Becket at the end of Part I of *Murder in the Cathedral*; also two of the poems they have published by Philip Larkin: *Annus Mirabilis* and *This be the Verse*.

Duff Hart-Davis for permission to publish *Father and Son: 1939*, by William Plomer;

David Higham Associates for permission to publish *To a Conscript of 1940*, by Sir Herbert Read;

Hodder and Stoughton Limited for permission to publish five poems by Sir John Betjeman: *The Planster's Vision, In a Bath Teashop, How To Get On In Society, Original Sin on the Sussex Coast* and *Death in Leamington*; © The Estate of John Betjeman 1955, 1958, 1960, 1962, 1964, 1966, 1970, 1979, 1980, 1981, 2001. Introduction Andrew Motion © 2006.

Johnson & Alcock Ltd for permission to publish *Warning*, by Jenny Joseph. Copyright © Jenny Joseph, Selected Poems.

The Barbara Levy Agency for permission to publish *The General* and *Everyone Sang*, both by Siegfried Sassoon.

PanMacmillan for permission to publish *Celia, Celia*, by Adrian Mitchell.

Peters, Fraser & Dunlop: Two poems by Hilaire Belloc, *The South Country* and *Henry King* are reprinted by permission of Peters Fraser & Dunlop (www.petersfraserdunlop.com), acting on behalf of the estate of Hilaire Belloc.

The Royal Literary Fund for permission to publish *Naming of Parts* and *Chard Whitlow, Mr Eliot's Sunday Evening Postscript*, both by Henry Reed.

The Society of Authors, as the Literary Representative of The Estate of Alfred Noyes, for permission to publish his poem *The Highwayman*; as the Literary Representative of the Estate of John Masefield, for permission to publish his poems *Cargoes* and *Sea Fever*; and as the Literary Trustees of Walter de la Mare, for permission to publish his poem *The Listeners*.

Sony/ATV Music Publihing (UK) Limited for permission to publish *The Lion and Albert*, Words and Music by George Marriott Edgar © 1933, Reproduced by permission of Francis Day & Hunter/ EMI Music Publishing Limited, London W1T 3LP.

Peter Southern, as Literary Executor for his father, Sir Richard Southern, for permission to quote the anonymous poem by a twelfth century nun of Auxerre, which appears on page 24 of Richard Southern's book, *The Making of the Middle Ages*.

Stainer & Bell Ltd, for permission to publish *Lord of the Dance* and *Friday Morning*, both by Sydney Carter, and also for permission to publish the quotation from Rabbi Lionel Blue's introduction to *Sydney Carter's Lord of the Dance and other songs and poems*.

United Agents for permission to publish *Valentine* by John Fuller.

Rights in **The Authorized (King James) Version** of the Bible are vested in the Crown in the United Kingdom, and quotations from that version are reproduced by permission of the Crown's patentee, **Cambridge University Press**. I am grateful to **CUP** for permission to publish two extracts from *The Authorized (King James) Version*: *David's Lament for Saul and Jonathan*, 2 Samuel Ch. 1, vv. 19–27, and verses 1-9 from Ch. 7 of *The Song of Solomon*.

Rights in **The Book of Common Prayer** are also vested in the Crown, and extracts are reproduced by permission of the Crown's patentee, **Cambridge University Press**. I am grateful to **CUP** for permission to quote three canticles, *Te Deum Laudamus*, *Magnificat* and *Nunc Dimittis*, and also twelve psalms from *The Book of Common Prayer.*

Apart from thanking those individuals and organisations who have given me permission to print poems whose copyright they hold, I would also like to express my appreciation of Tamsin Rush, Becky Banning and Julie Scott, all of Grosvenor House Publishing Limited, who between them saw this project through from conception to completion.

Finally my thanks go to my wife, Cathy, who found the picture of *Erato*, the Muse of Poetry, painted in 1870 by Sir Edward Poynter (1836 – 1919) and suggested it for the front cover, and who has also for years put up with me reciting poetry, either aloud or to myself, as we regularly walked together through the Sussex countryside.

David Arnold.
Horsham.   Summer 2021.

A List of the Contents Arranged Alphabetically by Authors.

Page

Anonymous

All abbesses deserve to die	3
I eat my peas with honey	74
My love in her attire doth show her wit	3
There was a young curate of Crediton	6
There was a young curate of Kew	6
There was a young poet called Spends	6
There was an old man of Japan	6
Western Wind, when will thou blow?	3

....

Mrs C.F.Alexander, 1818 – 1895

There is a green hill far away	138

St Ambrose, 339 – 397 (attributed to)

Te Deum Laudamus	19

W.H.Auden, 1907 – 1973

Funeral Blues	50
Note on Intellectuals	5

George Barker, 1913 – 1991

To my Mother	16

Hilaire Belloc, 1870 – 1953

Henry King	114
The South Country	170

John Betjeman, 1906 – 1984

Death in Leamington	128
How to get on in society	82
In a Bath Teashop	50
Original Sin on the Sussex Coast	127
The Planster's Vision	16

William Blake, 1757 – 1827

Jerusalem	136

Rupert Brooke, 1887 – 1915

The Soldier	65

Elizabeth Barrett Browning, 1806 – 1861

Sonnet from the Portuguese, XLIII	44

Robert Browning, 1812 – 1889
Home Thoughts from Abroad 191
Home Thoughts from the Sea 191
My last Duchess 165
Porphyria's Lover 106
John Bunyan, 1628 – 1688
To be a Pilgrim 135
Robert Burns, 1759 – 1796
John Anderson 41
To a Mouse, On Turning Her up in Her Nest
     with the Plough, November 1785 156
Thomas Campbell, 1777 – 1844
Lord Ullin's Daughter 88
Lewis Carroll, 1832 – 98
Father William 77
Jabberwocky 76
The Walrus and the Carpenter 108
Sydney Carter, 1915 – 2004
Friday Morning 146
Lord of the Dance 145
The Revd W. Chalmers Smith, 1824 – 1908
Immortal, invisible, God only wise 140
G.K.Chesterton, 1874 – 1936
The Donkey 193
A.H.Clough, 1819 – 1861
Say not the struggle nought availeth 139
Samuel Taylor Coleridge, 1772 – 1834
Kubla Khan 158
Wendy Cope, b.1945
After the Lunch 84
Another unfortunate choice 5
Bloody Men 83
Flowers 83
My Funeral 85
Two Cures for Love 5
Valentine 84

William Johnson Cory, 1823 – 1892
Heraclitus 44
King David, circa 1040 – 970 B.C., (attributed to)
Lament for Saul and Jonathan (2 *Samuel,*
Ch.1, vv. 19 – 27) 56
Psalms 1 Blessed is the man 21
8 O Lord our Governor 22
15 Lord, who shall dwell in thy
tabernacle 23
23 The Lord is my shepherd 24
46 God is our hope and strength 25
84 O how amiable are thy dwellings 26
95 O come, let us sing unto the Lord 27
100 O be joyful in the Lord 28
121 I will lift up mine eyes unto the hills 28
130 Out of the deep have I called unto thee 29
137 By the waters of Babylon 30
150 O praise God in his holiness 31
Keith Douglas, 1920 – 1944
Aristocrats: *'I think I am becoming a God'* 70
Vergissmeinicht 71
Michael Drayton, 1563 – 1631
Love's Farewell 9
George Marriott Edgar, 1880 – 1951
The Lion and Albert 121
T.S.Eliot, 1888 – 1965
Journey of the Magi 124
The Love Song of J. Alfred Prufrock 172
Thomas Becket's soliloquy at the end of Part I of
Murder in the Cathedral 177
John Fuller, b.1937
Valentine 51
George Herbert, 1593 – 1633
Love bade me welcome 35
Teach me, my God and King 133

Robert Herrick, 1591 – 1674
Carpe Diem   36
Whenas in silks my Julia goes   4
Thomas Hood, 1799 – 1845
I Remember, I Remember   189
A.E.Housman, 1859 – 1936
Loveliest of trees   192
Jenny Joseph, b.1932
Warning   81
John Keats, 1795 – 1821
La Belle Dame sans Merci   42
Ode on a Grecian Urn   160
Ode to a Nightingale   162
On first Looking into Chapman's Homer   13
Ode to Autumn   188
Rudyard Kipling, 1865 – 1936
If   167
The Roman Centurion's Song   168
Charles Lamb, 1775 – 1834
The Old Familiar Faces   187
Philip Larkin, 1922 – 1985
Annus Mirabilis   79
This be the verse   80
Edward Lear, 1812 – 1888
The Owl and the Pussycat   75
James Leigh Hunt, 1784 – 1859
Abou ben Adhem   90
Jenny kissed me   4
Henry Wadsworth Longfellow, 1807 – 1882
From *Tales of a Wayside Inn*: The Sicilian's Tale;
    King Robert of Sicily   99
Colonel Richard Lovelace, 1617 – 57
To Lucasta, Going to the Warres   57
Macaulay, Thomas Babington, 1ˢᵗ Baron, 1800 – 1859
Horatius (21 of 70 stanzas)   91

Walter de la Mare, 1873 – 1956
The Listeners   115
Andrew Marvell, 1621 – 1678
To his Coy Mistress   39
Mary of Nazareth (according to St Luke, Ch. 1, vv. 46 - 55)
Magnificat   20
John Masefield, 1868 – 1967
Cargoes   194
Sea Fever   194
Charlotte Mew, 1869 – 1928
The Farmer's Bride   112
Edna St Vincent Millay, 1892 – 1950
I being born a woman and distressed   15
If I should learn in some quite casual way   15
My candle burns at both ends   5
What lips my lips have kissed   14
John Milton, 1608 – 1674
Sonnet XVIII: On the late massacre in Piedmont   11
Sonnet XIX: On his blindness   11
Adrian Mitchell, 1932 – 2008
Celia, Celia   5
Sir Henry Newbolt, 1862 – 1938
Drake's Drum   62
Alfred Noyes, 1880 – 1958
The Highwayman   117
Wilfred Owen, 1893 – 1918
Anthem for Doomed Youth   65
Dulce Et Decorum Est   66
The Parable of the Old Man and the Young   126
William Plomer 1903 – 1973
Father and Son: 1939   179
Sir Herbert Read, 1893 – 1968
To a Conscript of 1940   67
Henry Reed, 1914 – 1986
Chard Whitlow   78
Naming of Parts   69

Rochester, the Earl of, 1647 – 1680
An extempore epitaph   74
Christina Rossetti, 1830 – 1894
In the Bleak Midwinter   141
Remember   13
The Russian Contakion of the Departed,
probably from the Byzantine Empire, 6ᵗʰ century A.D.   132
The Sarum Psalter, *a medieval Latin liturgy, translated
into English by the* **Revd G.H.Palmer, 1846 – 1926**
God be in my Head   132
Siegfied Sassoon, 1886 – 1967
Everyone Sang   64
The General   64
The Scottish Psalter of 1650
A metrical version of Psalm 23   134
Wiliam Shakespeare, 1564 – 1616
All the world's a stage (from *As You Like It,*
   Act 3, scene 7)   155
Fear no more the heat o' th' sun
   (from *Cymbeline, Act 4, scene 2)*   185
Henry V (*The Prologue*)   150
Henry V, Act 3, scene 1: *Henry V before Harfleur*   152
Henry V, Act 4, scene 3: *Henry V before Agincourt*   153
One sentence from John of Gaunt's dying speech
   in the first scene of *Richard II*   184
Sonnet XVIII: Shall I compare thee to a summer's day?   10
Sonnet CXVI: Let me not to the marriage of true minds   10
Percy Bysshe Shelley, 1792 – 1822
Ozymandias of Egypt   12
Simeon, quoted by St Luke, Ch.2, verses 29 - 32)
Nunc Dimittis   20
King Solomon, circa 990 – 931 B.C. (attributed to)
From *The Song of Solomon*, Ch.7, verses 1 - 9   34
Sir Cecil Spring Rice, 1859 – 1918
I vow to thee my country   143
Robert Louis Stevenson, 1850 – 1894
Requiem   193

Page

Alfred, Lord Tennyson, 1809 – 1892
Break, Break, Break   190
The Charge of the Light Brigade   60
Edward Thomas, 1878 – 1917
Adlestrop   63
No-one so much as you   48
Francis Thompson, 1859 – 1907
Daisy   45
In no strange land   144
Edmund Waller, 1606 – 1687
Song (Go, lovely Rose!)   37
On a Girdle   38
John G. Whittier 1807- 1893
Dear Lord and Father of Mankind   137
Charles Wolfe, 1791 – 1823
The Burial of Sir John Moore after Corunna   58
William Wordsworth, 1770 – 1850
Composed upon Westminster Bridge,
    September 3, 1802   12
The Daffodils   186
My heart leaps up when I behold a rainbow   4
William Butler Yeats, 1865 – 1933
Leda and the Swan   14
The Lake Isle of Innisfree   192

Section I

15 Short Poems

Fifteen Short Poems

Page 3

Western Wind	Anonymous
All Abbesses deserve to die	Anonymous
My love in her attire doth show her wit	Anonymous

Page 4

Whenas in silks my Julia goes	Robert Herrick, 1591 – 1674
My heart leaps up	William Wordsworth, 1770 – 1850
Jenny kissed me	James Leigh Hunt, 1784 – 1859

Page 5

My candle burns at both ends	Edna St Vincent Millay, 1892 – 1950
Note on Intellectuals	W H Auden, 1907 – 1973
Celia, Celia	Adrian Mitchell, 1932 – 2008
Two cures for love	Wendy Cope, b. 1945
Another unfortunate choice	Wendy Cope, b. 1945

Page 6

There was a young curate of Crediton	Anonymous
There was a young curate of Kew	Anonymous
There was a young poet called Spends	Anonymous
There was an old man of Japan	Anonymous

Here are two short poems from the Middle Ages, the first of which is well-known:

Western Wind (Anonymous)

Western wind, when will thou blow,
The small rain down can rain?
Christ, if my love were in my arms,
And I in my bed again!

The second is not widely known. It is quoted by the historian, Sir Richard Southern, in his book, The Making of the Middle Ages, *on page 24:*

All Abbesses deserve to die

All Abbesses deserve to die
Who order subject nuns to lie
In dire distress and lonely bed
Only for giving love its head.
I speak who know, for I've been fed,
For loving, long on stony bread.

Two more are from the seventeenth century:

My love in her attire (Anonymous)

My love in her attire doth show her wit,
It doth so well become her:
For every season she hath dressings fit,
For Winter, Spring, and Summer.

No beauty she doth miss
When all her robes are on:
But Beauty's self she is
When all her robes are gone.

Whenas in silks, by Robert Herrick, 1591 – 1674

Whenas in silks my Julia goes,
Then, then (methinks) how sweetly flows
The liquefaction of her clothes.

Next, when I cast mine eyes and see
That brave vibration each way free;
Oh how that glittering taketh me!

Two are from the early nineteenth century:

My heart leaps up by William Wordsworth, 1770 – 1850

My heart leaps up when I behold
   A rainbow in the sky:
So was it when my life began;
So is it now I am a man;
So be it when I shall grow old
   Or let me die!
The Child is father of the Man;
And I could wish my days to be
Bound each to each by natural piety.

Jenny kissed me by James Leigh Hunt, 1784 – 1859

Jenny kissed me when we met,
Jumping from the chair she sat in;
Time, you thief, who love to get
Sweets into your list, put that in!
Say I'm weary, say I'm sad,
Say that health and wealth have missed me,
Say I'm growing old, but add,
Jenny kissed me.

The others are all from the twentieth century:

My candle burns at both ends,
by Edna St Vincent Millay, 1892 – 1950

My candle burns at both ends.
It will not last the night;
But ah, my foes, and oh, my friends –
It gives a lovely light.

Note on Intellectuals, by W. H. Auden, 1907 – 1973

To the man-in-the-street, who, I'm sorry to say,
  Is a keen observer of life,
The word Intellectual suggests straight away
  A man who's untrue to his wife.

Celia, Celia, by Adrian Mitchell, 1932 – 2008

When I am sad and weary,
When I think all hope has gone,
When I walk along High Holborn
I think of you with nothing on.

Two cures for love, by Wendy Cope (b.1945)

1. Don't see him. Don't phone or write a letter.
2. The easy way: get to know him better.

Another Unfortunate Choice, by Wendy Cope (b. 1945)

I think I am in love with A.E. Housman,
Which puts me in a worse-than-usual-fix.
No woman ever stood a chance with Housman,
And he's been dead since 1936.

Finally, four of my favourite limericks – all, to the best of my belief, anonymous.

I like the first because of the rhyming of 'spread it on' and 'said it on' with 'Crediton':

There was a young curate of Crediton,
Who took *paté de foie gras* and spread it on
A chocolate biscuit and murmured 'I'll risk it.'
His tomb gives the date that he said it on.

The next only makes sense when one knows that the letter μ in Ancient Greek, the equivalent of our m, is pronounced 'Mew'.

There was a young curate of Kew,
Who, having nothing much else to do,
Taught his cat every week a new letter of Greek,
But never got further than μ.

These last two naturally go together:

There was a young poet called Spends,
Who said, 'All my poetry ends
Suddenly.'

and:

There was an old man of Japan,
Who could never make limericks scan.
When asked if he could, he replied, 'Well, I would,
But I always try to get as many words into the last line as
    I possibly can'.

Section II

15 Sonnets

Fifteen Sonnets

Page

1. Love's Farewell   Michael Drayton, 1563-1631   9

2. Shall I compare thee to a summer's day?
     William Shakespeare, 1564-1616   10

3. Let me not to the marriage of true minds
     William Shakespeare, 1564-1616   10

4. On his blindness   John Milton, 1608-74   11

5. On the late Massacre in Piedmont
     John Milton, 1608-74   11

6. Composed upon Westminster Bridge, 3rd Sept. 1802
     William Wordsworth, 1770-1850   12

7. Ozymandias   Percy Bysshe Shelley, 1792-1822   12

8. On first looking into Chapman's Homer
     John Keats, 1795-1821   13

9. Remember   Christina Rosetti, 1830-94   13

10. Leda and the Swan   William Butler Yeats,1865-1939   14

11. What lips my lips have kissed
     Edna St. Vincent Millay, 1892-1950   14

12. If I should learn   Edna St. Vincent Millay, 1892-1950   15

13. I, being born a woman
     Edna St. Vincent Millay, 1892-1950   15

14. The Planster's Vision   John Betjeman, 1906-82   16

15. To my Mother   George Barker, 1913-91   16

The sonnet is a particularly popular form with many poets. Shakespeare wrote at least 160, Wordsworth 523, and Keats 67 by the time he died at the age of twenty-five. Edna St Vincent Millay wrote 181.

A sonnet is almost always made up of fourteen lines of iambic pentameters, i.e. a line of ten syllables alternately unstressed and stressed, thus: 'Then slowly answered Arthur from the barge'. What is usually called a Shakespearean sonnet has a rhyme scheme ABAB CDCD EFEF GG, while what is called a Petrarchan sonnet typically has a first section of eight lines with the rhyme scheme ABBAABBA, followed by another six lines with the rhyme scheme CDE CDE.

The sonnet below by Michael Drayton has a rhyme scheme which clearly puts it in the Shakespearean category, but the division of its content into two very different sections, first an octet and then a sextet, make it feel more like a Petrarchan sonnet.

Love's Farewell, by Michael Drayton, 1563 – 1631

Since there's no help, come, let us kiss and part,-
Nay, I have done, you get no more of me,
And I am glad, yea, glad with all my heart,
That thus so cleanly I myself can free.
Shake hands for ever, cancel all our vows,
And when we meet at any time again,
Be it not seen in either of our brows
That we one jot of former love retain.
Now at the last gasp of Love's latest breath,
When, his pulse failing, Passion speechless lies,
When Faith is kneeling by his bed of death,
And Innocence is closing up his eyes,
Now, if thou wouldst, when all have giv'n him over,
From death to life thou might'st him yet recover.

Sonnet No. XVIII, by William Shakespeare, 1564 – 1616

Shall I compare thee to a summer's day?
Thou art more lovely and more temperate:
Rough winds do shake the darling buds of May,
And summer's lease hath all too short a date:
Sometime too hot the eye of heaven shines,
And often is his gold complexion dimm'd;
And every fair from fair sometime declines,
By chance, or nature's changing course, untrimm'd;
But thy eternal summer shall not fade
Nor lose possession of that fair thou ow'st;
Nor shall Death brag thou wander'st in his shade,
When in eternal lines to time thou grow'st;
So long as men can breathe or eyes can see,
So long lives this, and this gives life to thee.

Sonnet No. CXVI, by William Shakespeare, 1564 – 1616

Let me not to the marriage of true minds
Admit impediments. Love is not love
Which alters when it alteration finds,
Or bends with the remover to remove:
O, no! it is an ever-fixed mark,
That looks on tempests and is never shaken;
It is the star to every wandering bark,
Whose worth's unknown, although his height be taken.
Love's not Time's fool, though rosy lips and cheeks
Within his bending sickle's compass come;
Love alters not with his brief hours and weeks,
But bears it out even to the edge of doom.
If this be error, and upon me prov'd,
I never writ, nor no man ever lov'd.

Sonnet XIX: On his blindness, by John Milton, 1608 – 1674

When I consider how my light is spent
Ere half my days in this dark world and wide,
And that one talent which is death to hide
Lodg'd with me useless, though my soul more bent
To serve therewith my Maker, and present
My true account, lest he returning chide,–
"Doth God exact day-labour, light denied?"
I fondly ask. But Patience, to prevent
That murmur, soon replies: "God doth not need
Either man's work or his own gifts: who best
Bear his mild yoke, they serve him best. His state
Is kingly; thousands at his bidding speed
And post o'er land and ocean without rest:
They also serve who only stand and wait."

Sonnet XVIII: On the Late Massacre In Piedmont, also by Milton

Avenge, O Lord, thy slaughter'd saints, whose bones
Lie scatter'd on the Alpine mountains cold;
Ev'n them who kept thy truth so pure of old,
When all our fathers worshipp'd stocks and stones;
Forget not: in thy book record their groans
Who were thy sheep and in their ancient fold
Slain by the bloody Piedmontese that roll'd
Mother with infant down the rocks. Their moans
The vales redoubl'd to the hills, and they
To Heav'n. Their martyr'd blood and ashes sow
O'er all th' Italian fields where still doth sway
The triple tyrant; that from these may grow
A hundred-fold, who having learnt thy way
Early may fly the Babylonian woe.

*'The triple tyrant' is a reference to the three-tired papal crown, and
'the Babylonian woe' portrays the papacy as equivalent to Babylon.*

Composed Upon Westminster Bridge, September 3, 1802, by William Wordsworth, 1770 – 1850

Earth has not anything to show more fair:
Dull would he be of soul who could pass by
A sight so touching in its majesty:
This City now doth, like a garment, wear
The beauty of the morning; silent, bare.
Ships, towers, domes, theatres, and temples lie
Open unto the fields, and to the sky;
All bright and glittering in the smokeless air.
Never did sun more beautifully steep
In his first splendour valley, rock, or hill;
Ne'er saw I, never felt, a calm so deep!
The river glideth at his own sweet will:
Dear God! the very houses seem asleep;
And all that mighty heart is lying still!

Ozymandias of Egypt, by Percy Bysshe Shelley, 1792 – 1822

I met a traveller from an antique land,
Who said: "Two vast and trunkless legs of stone
Stand in the desert. Near them, on the sand,
Half sunk, a shattered visage lies, whose frown
And wrinkled lip and sneer of cold command,
Tell that its sculptor well those passions read
Which yet survive, stamped on these lifeless things,
The hand that mocked them, and the heart that fed;
And on the pedestal these words appear:
My name is Ozymandias, King of Kings;
Look on my Works, ye Mighty, and despair!
Nothing beside remains. Round the decay
Of that colossal wreck, boundless and bare,
The lone and level sands stretch far away."

On First Looking into Chapman's Homer, by John Keats, 1795 – 1821

Much have I travell'd in the realms of gold,
And many goodly states and kingdoms seen;
Round many western islands have I been
Which bards in fealty to Apollo hold.
Oft of one wide expanse had I been told
That deep-brow'd Homer ruled as his demesne;
Yet did I never breathe its pure serene
Till I heard Chapman speak out loud and bold:
Then felt I like some watcher of the skies
When a new planet swims into his ken;
Or like stout Cortez when with eagle eyes
He star'd at the Pacific—and all his men
Look'd at each other with a wild surmise—
Silent, upon a peak in Darien.

Remember, by Christina Rossetti, 1830 – 1894

Remember me when I am gone away,
Gone far away into the silent land;
When you can no more hold me by the hand,
Nor I half turn to go yet turning stay.
Remember me when no more day by day
You tell me of our future that you plann'd:
Only remember me; you understand
It will be late to counsel then or pray.
Yet if you should forget me for a while
And afterwards remember, do not grieve:
For if the darkness and corruption leave
A vestige of the thoughts that once I had,
Better by far you should forget and smile
Than that you should remember and be sad.

Leda and the Swan, by W.B.Yeats, 1865 – 1933

A sudden blow: the great wings beating still
Above the staggering girl, her thighs caressed
By the dark webs, her nape caught in his bill,
He holds her helpless breast upon his breast.
How can those terrified vague fingers push
The feathered glory from her loosening thighs?
And how can body, laid in that white rush,
But feel the strange heart beating where it lies?

A shudder in the loins engenders there
The broken wall, the burning roof and tower
And Agamemnon dead.
                                    Being so caught up,
So mastered by the brute blood of the air,
Did she put on his knowledge with his power
Before the indifferent beak could let her drop?

From *The Harp Weaver,* by Edna St Vincent Millay, 1892 – 1950

What lips my lips have kissed, and where, and why,
I have forgotten, and what arms have lain
Under my head till morning; but the rain
Is full of ghosts tonight, that tap and sigh
Upon the glass and listen for reply,
And in my heart there stirs a quiet pain
For unremembered lads that not again
Will turn to me at midnight with a cry.
Thus in winter stands the lonely tree,
Nor knows what birds have vanished one by one,
Yet knows its boughs more silent than before:
I cannot say what loves have come and gone,
I only know that summer sang in me
A little while, that in me sings no more.

14

From *Renascence*, by Edna St Vincent Millay, 1892 – 1950

If I should learn, in some quite casual way,
That you were gone, not to return again—
Read from the back-page of a paper, say,
Held by a neighbor in a subway train,
How at the corner of this avenue
And such a street (so are the papers filled)
A hurrying man—who happened to be you—
At noon to-day had happened to be killed,
I should not cry aloud—I could not cry
Aloud, or wring my hands in such a place—
I should but watch the station lights rush by
With a more careful interest on my face,
Or raise my eyes and read with greater care
Where to store furs and how to treat the hair.

Sonnet XLI, by Edna St. Vincent Millay, 1892 – 1950

I, being born a woman and distressed
By all the needs and notions of my kind,
Am urged by your propinquity to find
Your person fair, and feel a certain zest
To bear your body's weight upon my breast:
So subtly is the fume of life designed,
To clarify the pulse and cloud the mind,
And leave me once again undone, possessed.
Think not for this, however, the poor treason
Of my stout blood against my staggering brain,
I shall remember you with love, or season
My scorn with pity, —let me make it plain:
I find this frenzy insufficient reason
For conversation when we meet again.

The Planster's Vision, by John Betjeman, 1906 – 1984

Cut down that timber! Bells, too many and strong,
Pouring their music through the branches bare,
From moon-white church-towers down the windy air
Have pealed the centuries out with Evensong.
Remove those cottages, a huddled throng!
Too many babies have been born in there,
Too many coffins, bumping down the stair,
Carried the old their garden paths along.

I have a Vision of The Future, chum,
The worker's flats in fields of soya beans
Tower up like silver pencils, score on score:
And Surging Millions hear the Challenge come
From microphones in communal canteens
"No Right! No wrong! All's perfect, evermore."

To My Mother, by George Barker, 1913 – 1991

Most near, most dear, most loved and most far,
Under the window where I often found her
Sitting as huge as Asia, seismic with laughter,
Gin and chicken helpless in her Irish hand,
Irresistible as Rabelais, but most tender for
The lame dogs and hurt birds that surround her -
She is a procession no one can follow after
But be like a little dog following a brass band.

She will not glance up at the bomber, or condescend
To drop her gin and scuttle to a cellar,
But lean on the mahogany table like a mountain
Whom only faith can move, and so I send
O all my faith, and all my love to tell her
That she will move from mourning into morning.

Section III

15 Canticles
and Psalms

Fifteen Canticles and Psalms

Page

1. Te Deum Laudamus (We praise thee, O God) 19

2. Magnificat (My soul doth magnify the Lord) 20

3. Nunc Dimittis (Lord, now lettest thou thy servant depart in peace) 20

4. Psalm 1 (Blessed is the man) 21

5. Psalm 8 (O Lord our Governor) 22

6. Psalm 15 (Lord, who shall dwell in thy tabernacle?) 23

7. Psalm 23 (The Lord is my shepherd) 24

8. Psalm 46 (God is our hope and strength) 25

9. Psalm 84 (O how amiable are thy dwellings) 26

10. Psalm 95 (O come, let us sing unto the Lord) 27

11. Psalm 100 (O be joyful in the Lord, all ye lands) 28

12. Psalm 121 (I will lift up mine eyes unto the hills) 28

13. Psalm 130 (Out of the deep have I called unto thee, O Lord) 29

14. Psalm 137 (By the waters of Babylon we sat down and wept) 30

15. Psalm 150 (O praise God in his holiness) 31

Te Deum Laudamus(attributed to St Ambrose, 339 – 397),
which is usually sung at Matins in the Church of England.

We praise thee, O God, we acknowledge thee to be the Lord.

All the earth doth worship thee, the Father everlasting.

To thee all Angels cry aloud, the Heavens, and all the Powers
therein.

To thee Cherubim and Seraphim continually do cry, 'Holy, Holy,
Holy, Lord God of Sabaoth,

Heaven and earth are full of the Majesty of thy glory.'

The glorious company of the Apostles praise thee.

The goodly fellowship of the Prophets praise thee.

The noble army of Martyrs praise thee.

The holy Church throughout all the world doth acknowledge
thee, the Father, of an infinite Majesty, Thine honourable, true
and only Son, also the Holy Ghost, the Comforter.

Thou art the King of Glory, O Christ. Thou art the everlasting
Son of the Father.

When thou tookest upon thee to deliver man, thou didst not
abhor the Virgin's womb.

When thou hadst overcome the sharpness of death, thou didst
open the Kingdom of Heaven to all believers.

Thou sittest at the right hand of God in the glory of the Father.

We believe that thou shalt come to be our Judge.

We therefore pray thee, help thy servants, whom thou hast
redeemed with thy precious blood.

Make them to be numbered with thy Saints in glory everlasting.

O Lord, save thy people and bless thine heritage.

Govern them and lift them up for ever.

Day by day we magnify thee, and we worship thy Name, ever
world without end.

Vouchsafe, O Lord, to keep us this day without sin.

O Lord, have mercy upon us. Have mercy upon us.

O Lord, let thy mercy lighten upon us, as our trust is in thee.

O Lord, in thee have I trusted. Let me never be confounded.

*The **Magnificat**, which is to be found in the first chapter of St Luke's Gospel, and the **Nunc Dimittis**, which is from the second chapter, are both sung at Evensong.*

Magnificat, by Mary of Nazareth

My soul doth magnify the Lord, and my spirit hath rejoiced in God my Saviour, for he hath regarded the lowliness of His handmaid, for behold, from henceforth all generations shall call me blessed, for He that is mighty hath magnified me, and holy is His Name, and His mercy is on them that fear him throughout all generations.

He hath shewed strength with His arm. He hath scattered the proud in the imagination of their heart. He hath put down the mighty from their seat, and hath exalted the humble and meek. He hath filled the hungry with good things, and the rich he hath sent empty away.

He remembering his mercy hath holpen his servant Israel, as he promised to our forefathers, Abraham and his seed, for ever.

Nunc Dimittis, by Simeon

Lord, now lettest thou thy servant depart in peace, according to thy word, for mine eyes have seen thy salvation, which thou hast prepared before the face of all people, to be a light to lighten the Gentiles, and to be the glory of thy people Israel.

*They, as well as the **Te Deum** on the previous page, and also each of the psalms, are always followed in Anglican services by the words of the **Gloria**:*

Glory be to the Father and to the Son and to the Holy Ghost. As it was in the beginning, is now and ever shall be, world without end. Amen.

Psalm 1 (Beatus vir, qui non abiit)

Blessed is the man that hath not walked in the counsel of the ungodly, nor stood in the way of sinners, and hath not sat in the seat of the scornful.

But his delight is in the law of the Lord, and in his law will he exercise himself day and night.

And he shall be like a tree planted by the water-side, that will bring forth his fruit in due season.

His leaf also shall not wither, and look, whatsoever he doeth, it shall prosper.

As for the ungodly, it is not so with them, but they are like the chaff, which the wind scattereth away from the face of the earth.

Therefore the ungodly shall not be able to stand in the judgement, neither the sinners in the congregation of the righteous.

But the Lord knoweth the way of the righteous, and the way of the ungodly shall perish.

It is worth knowing that the law in which the blessed man is described as delighting is not simply a whole lot of legal instructions but rather the whole of the Pentateuch, the first five books of the Old Testament, which were often referred to by the ancient Hebrews as 'the Law'.

Psalm 8 (Domine, Dominus noster)

O Lord our Governor, how excellent is thy Name in all the world. Thou that has set thy glory above the heavens!

Out of the mouth of very babes and sucklings hast thou ordained strength, because of thine enemies, that thou mightest still the enemy, and the avenger.

For I will consider thy heavens, even the works of thy fingers, the moon and the stars, which thou hast ordained.

What is man, that thou art mindful of him, and the son of man, that thou visitest him?

Thou madest him lower than the angels, to crown him with glory and worship.

Thou makest him to have dominion of the works of thy hands, and thou hast put all things in subjection under his feet: all sheep and oxen, yea, and the beasts of the field, the fowls of the air, and the fishes of the sea, and whatsoever walketh through the paths of the seas.

O Lord our Governor, how excellent is thy Name in all the world!

Psalm 15 (Domine, quis habitabit?)

Lord, who shall dwell in thy tabernacle, or who shall rest upon thy holy hill?

Even he that leadeth an uncorrupt life, and doeth the thing which is right, and speaketh the truth from his heart.

He that hath used no deceit in his tongue, nor done evil to his neighbour, and hath not slandered his neighbour.

He that setteth not by himself, but is lowly in his own eyes, and maketh much of them that fear the Lord.

He that sweareth unto his neighbour, and disappointeth him not, though it were to his own hindrance.

He that hath not given his money upon usury, nor taken reward against the innocent.

Whoso doeth these things shall never fall.

Psalm 23 (*Dominus regit me*)

In the English-speaking world this is by far the best known of all the psalms, and it is known in a variety of translations (see, for example, the Scottish metrical version on page 134). It is worth noticing that it puts providing someone with food and drink before conversion and leading them into righteousness. That became and has remained characteristic of Jewish culture.

The Lord is my shepherd. Therefore can I lack nothing.

He shall feed me in a green pasture, and lead me forth beside the waters of comfort.

He shall convert my soul, and bring me forth in the paths of righteousness, for his Name's sake.

Yea, though I walk through the valley of the shadow of death, I will fear no evil, for thou art with me; thy rod and thy staff comfort me.

Thou shalt prepare a table before me against them that trouble me. Thou hast anointed my head with oil, and my cup shall be full.

But thy loving-kindness and mercy shall follow me all the days of my life, and I will dwell in the house of the Lord for ever.

Psalm 46 (Deus noster refugium)

God is our hope and strength, a very present help in trouble.

Therefore will we not fear, though the earth be moved, and though the hills be carried into the midst of the sea.

Though the waters thereof rage and swell, and though the mountains shake at the tempest of the same.

The rivers of the flood thereof shall make glad the city of God, the holy place of the tabernacle of the most Highest.

God is in the midst of her, therefore shall she not be removed. God shall help her, and that right early.

The heathen make much ado, and the kingdoms are moved, but God hath shewed his voice, and the earth shall melt away.

The Lord of hosts is with us. The God of Jacob is our refuge.

O come hither, and behold the works of the Lord, what destruction he hath brought upon the earth.

He maketh wars to cease in all the world. He breaketh the bow and knappeth the spear in sunder, and burneth the chariots in the fire.

Be still then, and know that I am God. I will be exalted among the heathen, and I will be exalted in the earth.

The Lord of hosts is with us. The God of Jacob is our refuge.

Psalm 84 (Quam dilecta!)

O how amiable are thy dwellings, thou Lord of hosts! My soul hath a desire and longing to enter into the courts of the Lord. My heart and my flesh rejoice in the living God.

Yea, the sparrow hath found her an house, and the swallow a nest where she may lay her young, even thy altars, O Lord of hosts, my King and my God.

Blessed are they that dwell in thy house. They will be alway praising thee. Blessed is the man whose strength is in thee, in whose heart are thy ways, who, going through the vale of misery, use it for a well, and the pools are filled with water.

They will go from strength to strength, and unto the God of gods appeareth every one of them in Sion. O Lord God of hosts, hear my prayer. Hearken, O God of Jacob.

Behold, O God our defender and look upon the face of thine Anointed, for one day in thy courts is better than a thousand.

I had rather be a door-keeper in the house of my God than to dwell in the tents of ungodliness.

For the Lord God is a light and defence. The Lord will give grace and worship, and no good thing shall he withhold from them that live a godly life.

O Lord God of hosts, blessed is the man that putteth his trust in thee.

Psalm 95 (Venite)

O come, let us sing unto the Lord; let us heartily rejoice in the strength of our salvation.

Let us come before his presence with thanksgiving, and shew ourselves glad in him with psalms.

For the Lord is a great God and a great King above all gods.

In his hand are all the corners of the earth, and the strength of the hills is his also.

The sea is his, and he made it, and his hands prepared the dry land.

O come, let us worship and fall down and kneel before the Lord our Maker.

For he is the Lord our God, and we are the people of his pasture, and the sheep of his hand.

To-day if ye will hear his voice, harden not your hearts, as in the provocation, and as in the day of temptation in the wilderness, when your fathers tempted me, proved me, and saw my works.

Forty years long was I grieved with this generation, and said, 'It is a people that do err in their hearts, for they have not known my ways, unto whom I sware in my wrath that they should not enter into my rest'.

Psalm 100 (Jubilate Deo)

O be joyful in the Lord, all ye lands; serve the Lord with gladness, and come before his presence with a song.

Be ye sure that the Lord he is God. It is he that hath made us, and not we ourselves; we are his people, and the sheep of his pasture.

O go your way into his gates with thanksgiving, and into his courts with praise. Be thankful unto him, and speak good of his Name.

For the Lord is gracious, his mercy is everlasting, and his truth endureth from generation to generation.

Psalm 121 (Levavi oculos)

I will lift up mine eyes unto the hills, from whence cometh my help.

My help cometh even from the Lord, who hath made heaven and earth.

He will not suffer thy foot to be moved, and he that keepeth thee will not sleep.

Behold, he that keepeth Israel shall neither slumber nor sleep.

The Lord himself is thy keeper. The Lord is thy defence upon thy right hand, so that the sun shall not burn thee by day, neither the moon by night.

The Lord shall preserve thee from all evil. Yea, it is even he that shall keep thy soul.

The Lord shall preserve thy going out and thy coming in, from this time forth for evermore.

Psalm 130 (De profundis)

Out of the deep have I called unto thee, O Lord. Lord, hear my voice.

O let thine ears consider well the voice of my complaint.

If thou, Lord, wilt be extreme to mark what is done amiss, O Lord, who may abide it?

For there is mercy with thee; therefore shalt thou be feared.

I look for the Lord; my soul doth wait for him; in his word is my trust.

My soul fleeth unto the Lord before the morning watch, I say, before the morning watch.

O Israel, trust in the Lord, for with the Lord there is mercy, and with him is plenteous redemption, and he shall redeem Israel from all his sins.

When Richard Collyer made his will in 1532, making arrangements for the foundation of what is now the College of Richard Collyer in Horsham, commonly known as Collyer's, where I spent sixteen years of my life, he asked that this psalm, the De profundis, *should be said at the departing of the school each day.*

One day in the late twentieth century I was asked by an inspector what our mission statement was. I told him that it was to say the De Profundis *for the soul of our founder, and his wife, Kateryn, and all Christian souls.*

Psalm 137 (Super flumina)

By the waters of Babylon we sat down and wept, when we remembered thee, O Sion.

As for our harps, we hanged them up upon the trees that are therein,

For they that led us away captive required of us then a song, and melody in our heaviness: ' Sing us one of the songs of Sion'.

'How shall we sing the Lord's song in a strange land?'

If I forget thee, O Jerusalem, let my right hand forget her cunning.

If I do not remember thee, let my tongue cleave to the roof of my mouth; yea if I prefer not Jerusalem in my mirth.

Remember the children of Edom, O Lord, in the day of Jerusalem, how they said, 'Down with it, down with it, even to the ground'.

O daughter of Babylon, wasted with misery, yea, happy shall he be that rewardeth thee as thou hast served us.

Blessed shall he be that taketh thy children and throweth them against the stones.

It is worth knowing that this psalm (clearly not by King David, since it refers to events long after his death) was written in three quite separate stages. The first four verses, which were written by someone who had experienced exile in Babylon, are some of the most beautiful words in the Bible. The next two verses are a commentary inspired by that and were written some years later. The last three verses, written many years after that, are some of the most unpleasant and vindictive sentiments in the whole of the Bible.

Psalm 150 (Laudate Dominum)

O praise God in his holiness; praise him in the firmament of his power.

Praise him in his noble acts; praise him according to his excellent greatness.

Praise him in the sound of the trumpet; praise him upon the lute and harp.

Praise him in the cymbals and dances; praise him upon the strings and pipe.

Praise him upon the well-tuned cymbals; praise him upon the loud cymbals.

Let everything that hath breath, praise the Lord.

This, the 150th, is the last of all the psalms, which between them comprise the longest book in the Old Testament. It is a resounding hymn of praise, and has been set to music by many composers. The setting by Charles Villiers Stanford is particularly beautiful.

Section IV

15 Poems on Aspects of Love

Fifteen Poems on Aspects of Love

		Page
1. From the Song of Solomon, Chapter 7, verses 1 – 9		34
2. Love Bade me Welcome	George Herbert, 1593 – 1633	35
3. *Carpe Diem*	Robert Herrick, 1591 – 1674	36
4. Song (Go, lovely Rose!)	Edmund Waller, 1606 – 1687	37
5. On a Girdle	also by Edmund Waller	38
6. To his Coy Mistress	Andrew Marvell, 1621 – 1678	39
7. John Anderson	Robert Burns, 1759 – 1796	41
8. *La Belle Dame sans Merci*	John Keats, 1795 – 1821	42
9. Sonnet from the Portuguese XLIII (How do I love thee?) Elizabeth Barrett Browning, 1806 – 1861		44
10. Heraclitus	William Johnson Cory, 1823 – 1892	44
11. Daisy	Francis Thompson, 1859 – 1907	45
12. No-one so much as you	Edward Thomas, 1878 – 1917	48
13. In a Bath Teashop	John Betjeman, 1906 – 1984	50
14. Funeral Blues	W.H.Auden, 1907 – 1973	50
15. Valentine	John Fuller, b.1937	51

Verses 1 – 9 of the seventh chapter of The Song of Solomon

How beautiful are thy feet with shoes, O prince's daughter! The joints of thy thighs are like jewels, the work of the hands of a cunning workman.

Thy navel is like a round goblet, which wanteth not liquor: thy belly is like an heap of wheat set about with lilies.

Thy two breasts are like two young roes that are twins.

Thy neck is as a tower of ivory; thine eyes like the fishpools in Heshbon, by the gate of Bathrabbim: thy nose is as the tower of Lebanon which looketh toward Damascus.

Thine head upon thee is like Carmel, and the hair of thine head like purple; the king is held in the galleries.

How fair and how pleasant art thou, O love, for delights!

This thy stature is like to a palm tree, and thy breasts to clusters of grapes.

I said, I will go up to the palm tree, I will take hold of the boughs thereof; now also thy breasts shall be as clusters of the vine, and the smell of thy nose like apples;

And the roof of thy mouth like the best wine for my beloved, that goeth down sweetly, causing the lips of those that are asleep to speak.

Love bade me welcome, by George Herbert, 1593 – 1633

Love bade me welcome: yet my soul drew back,
        Guilty of dust and sin.
But quick-ey'd Love, observing me grow slack,
        From my first entrance in,
Drew nearer to me, sweetly questioning,
        If I lack'd anything.

A guest, I answer'd, worthy to be here:
        Love said, You shall be he.
I the unkind, ungrateful? Ah my dear,
        I cannot look on thee.
Love took my hand, and smiling did reply,
        Who made the eyes but I?

Truth Lord, but I have marr'd them: let my shame
        Go where it doth deserve.
And know you not, says Love, who bore the blame?
        My dear, then I will serve.
You must sit down, says Love, and taste my meat:
        So I did sit and eat.

Carpe Diem (or To the Virgins, to Make Much of Time), by Robert Herrick, 1591 – 1674

Gather ye rose-buds while ye may,
Old Time is still a-flying;
And this same flower that smiles today
Tomorrow will be dying.

The glorious lamp of heaven, the sun,
The higher he's a-getting,
The sooner will his race be run,
And nearer he's to setting.

That age is best which is the first,
When youth and blood are warmer;
But being spent, the worse, and worst
Times still succeed the former.

Then be not coy, but use your time,
And while ye may, go marry;
For having lost but once your prime,
You may forever tarry.

Song (Go, lovely Rose!), by Edmund Waller, 1606 – 1687

Go, lovely Rose!
Tell her that wastes her time and me,
That now she knows,
When I resemble her to thee,
How sweet, and fair, she seems to be.

Tell her that's young,
And shuns to have her graces spy'd,
That hadst thou sprung
In deserts, where no men abide,
Thou must have uncommended dy'd.

Small is the worth
Of beauty from the light retir'd:
Bid her come forth,
Suffer her self to be desir'd,
And not blush so to be admir'd.

Then die! that she
The common fate of all things rare
May read in thee:
How small a part of time they share,
That are so wondrous sweet and faire!

On a Girdle, also by Edmund Waller

That which her slender waist confin'd,
Shall now my joyful temples bind;
  No monarch but would give his crown,
His arms might do what this has done.

It was my heaven's extremest sphere,
The pale which held that lovely deer:
  My joy, my grief, my hope, my love,
Did all within this circle move!

A narrow compass! and yet there
Dwelt all that's good, and all that's fair:
  Give me but what this ribbon bound,
Take all the rest the sun goes round.

By the time we left school, my twin brother and I had been together both at our elementary school and then, for another eight years, at Christ's Hospital. In the weeks after we left school and before we joined the army, knowing that I particularly liked these two poems by Edmund Waller, John bought me a leather-bound copy of The Works of Edmund Waller, Esq; *published by Mr. Fenton, London, MDCCXXX, with a note saying that it was in memory of our schooldays together. It is the oldest book I possess.*

To His Coy Mistress, by Andrew Marvell, 1621 – 78

Had we but world enough and time,
This coyness, lady, were no crime.
We would sit down and think which way
To walk and pass our long love's day.
Thou by the Indian Ganges' side
Shouldst rubies find; I by the tide
Of Humber would complain. I would
Love you ten years before the flood,
And you should, if you please, refuse
Till the conversion of the Jews.
My vegetable love should grow
Vaster than empires and more slow.
An hundred years should go to praise
Thine eyes, and on thy forehead gaze;
Two hundred to adore each breast,
But thirty thousand to the rest;
An age at least to every part,
And the last age should show your heart.
For, lady, you deserve this state,
Nor would I love at lower rate.

But at my back I always hear
Time's wingèd chariot hurrying near;
And yonder all before us lie
Deserts of vast eternity.
Thy beauty shall no more be found;
Nor, in my marble vault, shall sound
My echoing song; then worms shall try
That long-preserved virginity,
And your quaint honour turn to dust,
And into ashes all my lust.
The grave's a fine and private place,
But none, I think, do there embrace.

Now therefore, while the youthful hue
Sits on thy skin like morning dew,
And while thy willing soul transpires
At every pore with instant fires,
Now let us sport us while we may,
And now, like amorous birds of prey,
Rather at once our time devour
Than languish in his slow-chapt power.
Let us roll all our strength and all
Our sweetness up into one ball,
And tear our pleasures with rough strife
Through the iron gates of life:
Thus, though we cannot make our sun
Stand still, yet we will make him run.

John Anderson, by Robert Burns, 1759 – 96

John Anderson my jo, John,
  When we were first acquent,
Your locks were like the raven,
  Your bonny brow was brent;
But now your brow is beld, John,
  Your locks are like the snaw;
But blessings on your frosty pow,
  John Anderson my jo.

John Anderson my jo, John,
  We clamb the hill thegither
And mony a canty day, John,
  We've had wi' ane anither.
Now we maun totter down, John,
  And hand in hand we'll go,
And sleep thegither at the foot,
  John Anderson my jo!

La Belle Dame sans Merci, by John Keats, 1795 – 1821

O what can ail thee, knight-at-arms,
   Alone and palely loitering?
The sedge has withered from the lake,
   And no birds sing.

O what can ail thee, knight-at-arms,
   So haggard and so woe-begone?
The squirrel's granary is full,
   And the harvest's done.

I see a lily on thy brow,
   With anguish moist and fever-dew,
And on thy cheeks a fading rose
   Fast withereth too.

I met a lady in the meads,
   Full beautiful—a faery's child,
Her hair was long, her foot was light,
   And her eyes were wild.

I made a garland for her head,
   And bracelets too, and fragrant zone;
She looked at me as she did love,
   And made sweet moan

I set her on my pacing steed,
   And nothing else saw all day long,
For sidelong would she bend, and sing
   A faery's song.

She found me roots of relish sweet,
   And honey wild, and manna-dew,
And sure in language strange she said—
   'I love thee true'.

She took me to her elfin grot,
   And there she wept and sighed full sore,
And there I shut her wild wild eyes
   With kisses four.

And there she lulléd me asleep,
   And there I dreamed—Ah! Woe betide!—
The latest dream I ever dreamt
   On the cold hill side.

I saw pale kings and princes too,
   Pale warriors, death-pale were they all;
They cried—'La Belle Dame sans Merci
   Thee hath in thrall!'

I saw their starved lips in the gloam,
   With horrid warning gapéd wide,
And I awoke and found me here,
   On the cold hill's side.

And this is why I sojourn here,
   Alone and palely loitering,
Though the sedge is withered from the lake,
   And no birds sing.

Sonnet from the Portuguese XLIII,
by Elizabeth Barrett Browning, 1806 – 1861

How do I love thee? Let me count the ways.
I love thee to the depth and breadth and height
My soul can reach, when feeling out of sight
For the ends of being and ideal grace.
I love thee to the level of every day's
Most quiet need, by sun and candle-light.
I love thee freely, as men strive for right.
I love thee purely, as they turn from praise.

I love thee with the passion put to use
In my old griefs, and with my childhood's faith.
I love thee with a love I seemed to lose
With my lost saints. I love thee with the breath,
Smiles, tears, of all my life; and, if God choose,
I shall but love thee better after death.

Heraclitus, by W.J.Cory, 1823 – 92

They told me, Heraclitus, they told me you were dead,
They brought me bitter news to hear and bitter tears to shed.
I wept as I remembered how often you and I
Had tired the sun with talking and sent him down the sky.

And now that thou art lying, my dear old Carian* guest,
A handful of grey ashes, long, long ago at rest,
Still are thy pleasant voices, thy nightingales, awake;
For Death, he taketh all away, but these he cannot take.

*Heraclitus was a pre-Socratic philosopher from Ephesus in the area
of South-west Asia Minor known as Caria.
William Cory taught at Eton for twenty-seven years, from 1845 until
1872, when he was dismissed for encouraging friendly relationships
between masters and boys.

Daisy, by Francis Thompson, 1859 – 1907

Where the thistle lifts a purple crown
Six foot out of the turf,
And the harebell shakes on the windy hill--
O the breath of the distant surf!—

The hills look over on the South,
And southward dreams the sea;
And with the sea-breeze hand in hand
Came innocence and she.

Where 'mid the gorse the raspberry
Red for the gatherer springs,
Two children did we stray and talk
Wise, idle, childish things.

She listened with big-lipped surprise,
Breast-deep 'mid flower and spine,
Her skin was like a grape whose veins
Run snow instead of wine.

She knew not those sweet words she spake,
Nor knew her own sweet way;
But there's never a bird, so sweet a song
Thronged in whose throat all day.

Oh, there were flowers in Storrington
On the turf and on the spray;
But the sweetest flower on Sussex hills
Was the Daisy-flower that day!

Her beauty smoothed earth's furrowed face.
She gave me tokens three:–
A look, a word of her winsome mouth,
And a wild raspberry.

A berry red, a guileless look,
A still word,–strings of sand!
And yet they made my wild, wild heart
Fly down to her little hand.

For standing artless as the air,
And candid as the skies,
She took the berries with her hand,
And the love with her sweet eyes.

The fairest things have fleetest end,
Their scent survives their close:
But the rose's scent is bitterness
To him that loved the rose.

She looked a little wistfully,
Then went her sunshine way: -
The sea's eye had a mist on it,
And the leaves fell from the day.

She went her unremembering way;
She went and left in me
The pang of all the partings gone,
And partings yet to be.

She left me marvelling why my soul
Was sad that she was glad;
At all the sadness in the sweet,
The sweetness in the sad.

Still, still I seemed to see her, still
Look up with soft replies,
And take the berries with her hand,
And the love with her lovely eyes.

Nothing begins, and nothing ends,
That is not paid with moan;
For we are born in other's pain,
And perish in our own.

No one so much as you, by Edward Thomas, 1878 – 1917

No one so much as you
Loves this my clay,
Or would lament as you
Its dying day.

You know me through and through
Though I have not told,
And though with what you know
You are not bold.

None ever was so fair
As I thought you:
Not a word can I bear
Spoken against you.

All that I ever did
For you seemed coarse
Compared with what I hid
Nor put in force.

My eyes scarce dare meet you
Lest they should prove
I but respond to you
And do not love.

We look and understand,
We cannot speak
Except in trifles and
Words the most weak.

For I at most accept
Your love, regretting
That is all: I have kept
Only a fretting

That I could not return
All that you gave
And could not ever burn
With the love you have,

Till sometimes it did seem
Better it were
Never to see you more
Than linger here

With only gratitude
Instead of love -
A pine in solitude
Cradling a dove.

In A Bath Teashop, by John Betjeman, 1906 – 84

"Let us not speak, for the love we bear one another—
Let us hold hands and look."
She such a very ordinary little woman;
He such a thumping crook;
But both, for a moment, little lower than the angels
In the teashop's ingle-nook.

Funeral Blues, by W.H.Auden, 1907 – 73

Stop all the clocks, cut off the telephone,
Prevent the dog from barking with a juicy bone,
Silence the pianos and with muffled drum
Bring out the coffin, let the mourners come.

Let aeroplanes circle moaning overhead
Scribbling on the sky the message 'He is Dead'.
Put crepe bows round the white necks of the public doves,
Let the traffic policemen wear black cotton gloves.

He was my North, my South, my East and West,
My working week and my Sunday rest,
My noon, my midnight, my talk, my song;
I thought that love would last forever: I was wrong.

The stars are not wanted now; put out every one;
Pack up the moon and dismantle the sun;
Pour away the ocean and sweep up the wood,
For nothing now can ever come to any good.

Valentine, by John Fuller, born 1937

The things about you I appreciate
may seem indelicate:
I'd like to find you in the shower
and chase the soap for half an hour.
I'd like to have you in my power
and see your eyes dilate.
I'd like to have your back to scour
and other parts to lubricate.
Sometimes I feel it is my fate
to chase you screaming up a tower
or make you cower
by asking you to differentiate
Nietzsche from Schopenhauer.
I'd like successfully to guess your weight
and win you at a fete.
I'd like to offer you a flower.

I like the hair upon your shoulders
falling like water over boulders.
I like the shoulders, too: they are essential.
Your collar-bones have great potential
(I'd like all your particulars in folders
marked *Confidential*).

I like your cheeks, I like your nose,
I like the way your lips disclose
the neat arrangement of your teeth
(Half above and half beneath)
In rows.

I like your eyes, I like their fringes.
The way they focus on me gives me twinges.
Your upper arms drive me berserk
I like the way your elbows work,
On hinges.

I like your wrists, I like your glands,
I like the fingers on your hands.
I'd like to teach them how to count,
And certain things we might exchange,
Something familiar for something strange.
I'd like to give you just the right amount
And get some change.

I like it when you tilt your cheek up.
I like the way you hold a teacup.
I like your legs when you unwind them.
Even in trousers I don't mind them.
I like each softly moulded kneecap.
I like the little crease behind them.
I'd always know, without a recap,
Where to find them.

I like the sculpture of your ears.
I like the way your profile disappears
Whenever you decide to turn and face me.
I'd like to cross two hemispheres
And have you chase me.
I'd like to smuggle you across frontiers
Or sail with you at night into Tangiers.
I'd like you to embrace me.

I'd like to see you ironing your skirt
And cancelling other dates,
I'd like to button up your shirt.
I like the way your chest inflates.
I'd like to soothe you when you're hurt
Or frightened senseless by invertebrates.

I'd like you even if you were malign
And had a yen for sudden homicide.
I'd let you put insecticide
Into my wine.
I'd even like you if you were the Bride of Frankenstein
Or something ghoulish out of Mamoulian's Jekyll and
    Hyde.

52

I'd even like you as my Julian
Of Norwich or Cathleen ni Houlihan.
How melodramatic
If you were something muttering in attics
    Like Mrs Rochester or a student of Boolean Mathematics.

You are the end of self-abuse.
You are the eternal feminine.
I'd like to find a good excuse
To call on you and find you in.
I'd like to put my hand beneath your chin,
And see you grin.
I'd like to taste your Charlotte Russe,
I'd like to feel my lips upon your skin,
I'd like to make you reproduce.

I'd like you in my confidence.
I'd like to be your second look.
I'd like to let you try the French Defence
And mate you with my rook.
I'd like to be your preference
And hence
I'd like to be around when you unhook.
I'd like to be your only audience,
The final name in your appointment book,
Your future tense.

John Fuller became a Fellow of Magdalen College, Oxford, in 1966 at the age of twenty-nine and taught English Literature there for the next thirty-six years. He is now a Fellow Emeritus.

In Valentine *he captures the obsessive nature of the feelings of a man who has fallen in love better than in any poem since Andrew Marvell's* To His Coy Mistress *(on pages 39 and 40).*

Section V

15 Poems about War and Peace

Fifteen Poems about War and Peace

		Page
1.	David's Lament for Saul and Jonathan, 2 Samuel, Chapter 1, verses 19 – 27	56
2.	To Lucasta, Going to the Warres by Colonel Lovelace, 1617 – 1657	57
3.	The Burial of Sir John Moore after Corunna by Charles Wolfe, 1791 – 1823	58
4.	The Charge of the Light Brigade by Alfred, Lord Tennyson, 1809 – 92	60
5.	Drake's Drum by Sir Henry Newbolt, 1862 – 1938	62
6.	Adlestrop by Edward Thomas, 1878 – 1917	63
7.	The General by Siegfried Sassoon, 1886 – 1967	64
8.	Everyone Sang by Siegfied Sassoon, 1886 – 1967	64
9.	The Soldier by Rupert Brooke, 1887 – 1915	65
10.	Anthem for Doomed Youth by Wilfred Owen, 1893 – 1918	65
11.	*Dulce Et Decorum Est* by Wilfred Owen, 1893 – 1918	66
12.	To a Conscript of 1940 by Sir Herbert Read, 1893 – 1968	67
13.	Lessons of the War by Henry Reed, 1914 – 1986	68/69
14.	Aristocrats by Keith Douglas, 1920 – 1944	70
15.	*Vergissmeinicht* by Keith Douglas, 1920 – 1944	71

David's Lament for Saul and Jonathan

This is taken from the Second Book of Samuel of the ancient Jewish scriptures, as translated in the King James Bible, chapter 1, verses 19–27. The punctuation has been up-dated to meet the conventions of the early twenty-first century. There are no other changes.

The beauty of Israel is slain upon thy high places. How are the mighty fallen!

Tell it not in Gath, publish it not in the streets of Askelon, lest the daughters of the Philistines rejoice, lest the daughters of the uncircumcised triumph.

Ye mountains of Gilboa, let there be no dew, neither let there be rain upon you, nor fields of offerings, for there the shield of the mighty is vilely cast away, the shield of Saul, as though he had not been anointed with oil.

From the blood of the slain, from the fat of the mighty, the bow of Jonathan turned not back and the sword of Saul returned not empty.

Saul and Jonathan were lovely and pleasant in their lives, and in their death they were not divided. They were swifter than eagles, they were stronger than lions.

Ye daughters of Israel, weep over Saul, who clothed you in scarlet, with other delights, who put on ornaments of gold upon your apparel.

How are the mighty fallen in the midst of the battle! O Jonathan, thou was slain in thine high places.

I am distressed for thee, my brother Jonathan. Very pleasant hast thou been unto me. Thy love to me was wonderful, passing the love of women.

How are the mighty fallen, and the weapons of war perished!

To Lucasta, Going to the Warres,
by Colonel Richard Lovelace, 1617 – 1657

Tell me not (Sweet) I am unkinde,
That from the Nunnerie
Of thy chaste breast and quiet minde,
To Warre and Armes I flie.

True; A new Mistresse now I chase,
The first Foe in the Field;
And with a stronger Faith imbrace
A Sword, a Horse, a Shield.

Yet this Inconstancy is such
As you too shall adore;
I could not love thee (Deare) so much,
Lov'd I not Honour more.

The Burial of Sir John Moore after Corunna (1809), by Charles Wolfe, 1791 – 1823

Not a drum was heard, not a funeral note,
As his corpse to the rampart we hurried;
Not a soldier discharged his farewell shot
O'er the grave where our hero we buried.

We buried him darkly at dead of night,
The sods with our bayonets turning;
By the struggling moonbeam's misty light
And the lantern dimly burning.

No useless coffin enclosed his breast,
Not in sheet or in shroud we wound him,
But he lay like a warrior taking his rest
With his martial cloak around him.

Few and short were the prayers we said,
And we spoke not a word of sorrow;
But we steadfastly gazed on the face that was dead,
And we bitterly thought of the morrow.

We thought, as we hollowed his narrow bed
And smoothed down his lonely pillow,
That the foe and the stranger would tread o'er his head,
And we far away on the billow!

Lightly they'll talk of the spirit that's gone
And o'er his cold ashes upbraid him,
But little he'll reck, if they let him sleep on
In the grave where a Briton has laid him.

But half of our heavy task was done
When the clock struck the hour for retiring;
And we heard the distant and random gun
That the foe was sullenly firing.

Slowly and sadly we laid him down,
From the field of his fame fresh and gory;
We carved not a line, and we raised not a stone,
But we left him alone with his glory.

The Charge of the Light Brigade, by Alfred, Lord Tennyson, 1809 – 92

The charge of the Light Brigade at Balaclava in the Crimea in 1854 is nowadays thought of as a disaster. Tennyson's poem celebrates it.

Half a league, half a league,
Half a league onward,
All in the valley of Death
  Rode the six hundred.
"Forward, the Light Brigade!
Charge for the guns!" he said.
Into the valley of Death
  Rode the six hundred.

"Forward, the Light Brigade!"
Was there a man dismayed?
Not though the soldier knew
  Someone had blundered.
  Theirs not to make reply,
  Theirs not to reason why,
  Theirs but to do and die.
  Into the valley of Death
  Rode the six hundred.

Cannon to right of them,
Cannon to left of them,
Cannon in front of them
  Volleyed and thundered;
Stormed at with shot and shell,
Boldly they rode and well,
Into the jaws of Death,
Into the mouth of Hell
  Rode the six hundred.

Flashed all their sabres bare,
Flashed as they turned in air
Sabring the gunners there,
Charging an army, while
  All the world wondered.
Plunged in the battery-smoke
Right through the line they broke;
Cossack and Russian
Reeled from the sabre stroke
  Shattered and sundered.
Then they rode back, but not,
  Not the six hundred.

Cannon to right of them,
Cannon to left of them,
Cannon behind them
  Volleyed and thundered;
Stormed at with shot and shell,
While horse and hero fell,
They that had fought so well
Came through the jaws of Death,
Back from the mouth of Hell,
All that was left of them,
  Left of six hundred.

When can their glory fade?
O the wild charge they made!
  All the world wondered.
Honour the charge they made!
Honour the Light Brigade,
  Noble six hundred!

Drake's Drum, by Sir Henry Newbolt, 1862 – 1938

Drake he's in his hammock an' a thousand miles away,
(Capten, art tha sleepin' there below?)
Slung atween the round shot in Nombre Dios Bay,
An' dreamin' arl the time o' Plymouth Hoe.
Yarnder lumes the Island, yarnder lie the ships,
Wi' sailor lads a-dancin' heel-an'-toe,
An' the shore-lights flashin', an' the night-tide dashin',
He sees et arl so plainly as he saw et long ago.

Drake he was a Devon man, an' rüled the Devon seas,
(Capten, art tha' sleepin' there below?)
Roving' tho' his death fell, he went wi' heart at ease,
A' dreamin' arl the time o' Plymouth Hoe.
"Take my drum to England, hang et by the shore,
Strike et when your powder's runnin' low;
If the Dons sight Devon, I'll quit the port o' Heaven,
An' drum them up the Channel as we drumm'd them long ago."

Drake he's in his hammock till the great Armadas come,
(Capten, art tha sleepin' there below?)
Slung atween the round shot, listenin' for the drum,
An' dreamin arl the time o' Plymouth Hoe.
Call him on the deep sea, call him up the Sound,
Call him when ye sail to meet the foe;
Where the old trade's plyin' an' the old flag flyin'
They shall find him ware an' wakin', as they found him
    long ago!

Adlestrop, by Edward Thomas, 1878 – 1917

Other English poets of the First World War wrote of the tragedy of war and the pity of war. Edward Thomas, who was old enough not to need to go to war, chose to enlist and served in the Royal Artillery. When he wrote poetry, he wrote of the English countryside, which he loved and for which he felt he was fighting.

He was killed in 1917 at the end of the Battle of Arras, which is referred to in Siegfried Sassoon's poem The General *on the next page.*

Yes, I remember Adlestrop -
The name, because one afternoon
Of heat the express-train drew up there
Unwontedly. It was late June.

The steam hissed. Someone cleared his throat.
No one left and no one came
On the bare platform. What I saw
Was Adlestrop – only the name

And willows, willow-herb, and grass,
And meadowsweet, and haycocks dry,
No whit less still and lonely fair
Than the high cloudlets in the sky.

And for that minute a blackbird sang
Close by, and around him, mistier,
Farther and farther, all the birds
Of Oxfordshire and Gloucestershire.

The General, by Siegfried Sassoon, 1886 – 1967

"Good-morning, good-morning!" the General said
When we met him last week on our way to the line.
Now the soldiers he smiled at are most of 'em dead,
And we're cursing his staff for incompetent swine.

"He's a cheery old card," grunted Harry to Jack
As they slogged up to Arras with rifle and pack.

………..

But he did for them both by his plan of attack.

Everyone Sang, also by Siegfried Sassoon

*This was written as a celebration of
the Armistice on 11th November 1918.*

Everyone suddenly burst out singing;
And I was filled with such delight
As prisoned birds must find in freedom,
Winging wildly across the white
Orchards and dark-green fields; on; on; and out of sight.

Everyone's voice was suddenly lifted;
And beauty came like the setting sun:
My heart was shaken with tears; and horror
Drifted away ... O, but every one
Was a bird; and the song was wordless; the singing will never
   be done.

The Soldier, by Rupert Brooke, 1887 – 1915

If I should die, think only this of me:
  That there's some corner of a foreign field
That is for ever England. There shall be
  In that rich earth a richer dust concealed;
A dust whom England bore, shaped, made aware,
  Gave, once, her flowers to love, her ways to roam,
A body of England's breathing English air,
  Washed by the rivers, blest by suns of home.

And think, this heart, all evil shed away,
  A pulse in the eternal mind, no less,
    Gives somewhere back the thoughts by England given;
Her sights and sounds; dreams happy as her day;
  And laughter, learnt of friends; and gentleness,
    In hearts at peace, under an English heaven.

Anthem for Doomed Youth, by Wilfred Owen, 1893 – 1918

What passing-bells for these who die as cattle?
Only the monstrous anger of the guns.
Only the stuttering rifles' rapid rattle
Can patter out their hasty orisons.
No mockeries now for them; no prayers nor bells;
Nor any voice of mourning save the choirs, –
The shrill, demented choirs of wailing shells;
And bugles calling for them from sad shires.

What candles may be held to speed them all?
Not in the hands of boys but in their eyes
Shall shine the holy glimmers of goodbyes.
The pallor of girls' brows shall be their pall;
Their flowers the tenderness of patient minds,
And each slow dusk a drawing-down of blinds.

Dulce Et Decorum Est, by Wilfrid Owen, 1893 – 1918

Bent double, like old beggars under sacks,
Knock-kneed, coughing like hags, we cursed through sludge,
Till on the haunting flares we turned our backs
And towards our distant rest began to trudge.
Men marched asleep. Many had lost their boots
But limped on, blood-shod. All went lame; all blind;
Drunk with fatigue; deaf even to the hoots
Of tired, outstripped Five-Nines that dropped behind.

Gas! Gas! Quick, boys! – An ecstasy of fumbling,
Fitting the clumsy helmets just in time;
But someone still was yelling out and stumbling,
And flound'ring like a man in fire or lime . . .
Dim, through the misty panes and thick green light,
As under a green sea, I saw him drowning.

In all my dreams, before my helpless sight,
He plunges at me, guttering, choking, drowning.

If in some smothering dreams you too could pace
Behind the wagon that we flung him in,
And watch the white eyes writhing in his face,
His hanging face, like a devil's sick of sin;
If you could hear, at every jolt, the blood
Come gargling from the froth-corrupted lungs,
Obscene as cancer, bitter as the cud
Of vile, incurable sores on innocent tongues,
My friend, you would not tell with such high zest
To children ardent for some desperate glory,
The old Lie; *Dulce et decorum est*
Pro patria mori.

To A Conscript of 1940, by Sir Herbert Read, 1893 – 1968

A soldier passed me in the freshly fallen snow,
His footsteps muffled, his face unearthly grey:
And my heart gave a sudden leap
As I gazed on a ghost of five-and-twenty years ago.

I shouted Halt! and my voice had the old accustom'd ring
And he obeyed it as it was obeyed
In the shrouded days when I too was one
Of an army of young men marching

Into the unknown. He turned towards me and I said:
'I am one of those who went before you
Five-and-twenty years ago: one of the many who never returned,
Of the many who returned and yet were dead.

We went where you are going, into the rain and the mud:
We fought as you will fight
With death and darkness and despair;
We gave what you will give – our brains and our blood.

We think we gave in vain. The world was not renewed.
There was hope in the homestead and anger in the streets,
But the old world was restored and we returned
To the dreary field and workshop, and the immemorial feud

Of rich and poor. Our victory was our defeat.
Power was retained where power had been misused
And youth was left to sweep away
The ashes that the fires had strewn beneath our feet.

But one thing we learned: there is no glory in the dead
Until the soldier wears a badge of tarnish'd braid;
There are heroes who have heard the rally and have seen
The glitter of garland round their head.

Theirs is the hollow victory. They are deceived.
But you my brother and my ghost, if you can go
Knowing that there is no reward, no certain use
In all your sacrifice, then honour is reprieved.

To fight without hope is to fight with grace,
The self reconstructed, the false heart repaired.'
Then I turned with a smile, and he answered my salute
As he stood against the fretted hedge, which was like white lace.

Naming of Parts, by Henry Reed, 1914 – 86

The poem on the next page is by Henry Reed, who was twenty-seven when he was conscripted into the army in the summer of 1941. His basic training inspired the three poems which are grouped together as Lessons of the War, *and of which the best known is this one*: Naming of Parts. *As a preface to the poem Reed misquotes, no doubt deliberately, the beginning of one of Horace's* Odes *(III.26). Horace had written* Vixi puellis nuper idoneus et militavi non sine gloria. *Reed alters one letter, changing* puellis *to* duellis, *an old and little-used Latin word for war, or conflict. The original can be loosely translated like this: 'Recently I have lived my life for girls and have struggled with them not without glory'. Why, and with what significance, he changed* puellis *to* duellis *anyone can guess.*

Anyone who did his basic training during the Second World War, or later, at the start of National Service, will recognise the voices of the N.C.O. instructor and the recruit.

Naming of Parts, by Henry Reed, 1914 – 86

Today we have naming of parts. Yesterday
We had daily cleaning. And tomorrow morning,
We shall have what to do after firing. But today,
Today we have naming of parts. Japonica
Glistens like coral in all of the neighbouring gardens,
And today we have naming of parts.

This is the lower sling swivel. And this
Is the upper sling swivel, whose use you will see,
When you are given your slings. And this is the piling swivel,
Which in your case you have not got. The branches
Hold in the gardens their silent, eloquent gestures,
Which in our case we have not got.

This is the safety-catch, which is always released
With an easy flick of the thumb. And please do not let me
See anyone using his finger. You can do it quite easy
If you have any strength in your thumb. The blossoms
Are fragile and motionless, never letting anyone see
Any of them using their finger.

And this you can see is the bolt. The purpose of this
Is to open the breech, as you see. We can slide it
Rapidly backwards and forwards; we call this
Easing the spring. And rapidly backwards and forwards
The early bees are assaulting and fumbling the flowers:
They call it easing the Spring.

They call it easing the Spring. It is perfectly easy
If you have any strength in your thumb; like the bolt,
And the breech, and the cocking piece, and the point of balance,
Which in our case we have not got; and the almond-blossom
Silent in all of the gardens and the bees going backwards
    and forwards,
For today we have naming of parts.

Aristocrats: "*I think I am becoming a God*", by Keith Douglas, 1920 – 1944

The noble horse with courage in his eye
clean in the bone, looks up at a shellburst:
away fly the images of the shires
but he puts the pipe back in his mouth.

Peter was unfortunately killed by an 88;
it took his leg away, he died in the ambulance.
I saw him crawling on the sand, he said
It's most unfair, they've shot my foot off.

How can I live among this gentle
obsolescent breed of heroes, and not weep?
Unicorns, almost,
for they are falling into two legends
in which their stupidity and chivalry
are celebrated. Each, fool and hero, will be an immortal.

The plains were their cricket pitch
and in the mountains the tremendous drop fences
brought down some of the runners. Here then
under the stones and earth they dispose themselves,
I think with their famous unconcern.
It is not gunfire I hear, but a hunting horn.

I first came across the poetry of Keith Douglas in the winter of 1951-1952, when David Roberts, who taught both of us at Christ's Hospital, lent me a copy of Douglas's recently published Selected Poems. *We had played in the same position in the school 1st XV and had won the same History prize. But he was a veteran of desert warfare when he was killed at the age of twenty-four on 9th June 1944, four days after D-Day, shortly before I arrived at the school.*

Vergissmeinicht, **also by Keith Douglas.**

Three weeks gone and the combatants gone,
returning over the nightmare ground
we found the place again, and found
the soldier sprawling in the sun.

The frowning barrel of his gun
overshadowing. As we came on
that day, he hit my tank with one
like the entry of a demon.

Look. Here in the gunpit spoil
the dishonoured picture of his girl
who has put: *Steffi. Vergissmeinicht*
in a copybook gothic script.

We see him almost with content
abased, and seeming to have paid
and mocked at by his own equipment
that's hard and good when he's decayed.

But she would weep to see today
how on his skin the swart flies move;
the dust upon the paper eye
and the burst stomach like a cave.

For here the lover and killer are mingled
who had one body and one heart.
And death who had the soldier singled
has done the lover mortal hurt.

Years later I found Douglas's grave in the military cemetery at Tilly-sur-Seulles in Normandy (plot no.1, row E, grave no.2). The inscription on it is 'These things' he loved. He died in their defence. It is a reference to verse 8, Ch. 4, of Paul's letter to the Philippians, which Douglas had heard each year on Founder's Day at school.

Section VI

15 Examples of Comic and Amusing Verse

Fifteen Examples of Comic
and Amusing verse.

Page

1. I eat my peas with honey, Anonymous.   74

2. An extempore epitaph by John Wilmot,
    the second Earl of Rochester, 1647 - 1680   74

3. The Owl and the Pussy-cat by Edward Lear,
    1812 – 1888   75

4. Jabberwocky by Lewis Carroll, 1832 – 1898   76

5. Father William by Lewis Carroll, 1832 – 1898   77

6. Chard Whitlow by Henry Reed, 1914 – 1986   78

7. *Annus Mirabilis* by Philip Larkin, 1922 – 1985   79

8. This be the verse by Philip Larkin, 1922 – 1985   80

9. Warning by Jenny Joseph, b. 1932   81

10. How to get on in Society by John Betjeman,
    1906 – 1984   82

11. Bloody Men by Wendy Cope, b. 1945   83

12. Flowers by Wendy Cope, b. 1945   83

13. After the Lunch by Wendy Cope, b. 1945   84

14. Valentine by Wendy Cope, b. 1945   84

15. My Funeral by Wendy Cope, b. 1945   85

I eat my peas with honey (Anonymous).

This is the first comic poem I can remember enjoying as a child. Its anonymity makes it difficult to place in a group of poems arranged chronologically, and it should probably go somewhat later, but for convenience I have placed it at the beginning of this section:

> I eat my peas with honey.
> I've done it all my life.
> It makes the peas taste funny,
> But it keeps them on the knife.

Its particular appeal to me as a child was because I found it difficult to keep peas on the back of a fork, which was, I was told, the only polite way to eat them.

**An extempore epitaph on Charles II,
by the Earl of Rochester, 1647 – 1680**

The following four lines were apparently produced impromptu by the young courtier, John Wilmot, 2ⁿᵈ Earl of Rochester, when challenged by King Charles II to provide an epitaph for him:

> Here lies a great and mighty king,
> Whose word no man relies on,
> Who never said a foolish thing,
> Nor ever did a wise one.

Charles is reputed to have replied, equally impromptu: My words are my own. My deeds are my ministers'.

The Owl and the Pussy-cat, by Edward Lear, 1812 – 88

The Owl and the Pussy-cat went to sea
 In a beautiful pea-green boat,
They took some honey, and plenty of money,
 Wrapped up in a five-pound note.
The Owl looked up to the stars above,
 And sang to a small guitar,
"O lovely Pussy! O Pussy, my love,
 What a beautiful Pussy you are,
  You are,
  You are!
What a beautiful Pussy you are!"

Pussy said to the Owl, "You elegant fowl!
 How charmingly sweet you sing!
O let us be married! too long we have tarried:
 But what shall we do for a ring?"
They sailed away, for a year and a day,
 To the land where the Bong-Tree grows
And there in a wood a Piggy-wig stood
 With a ring at the end of his nose,
  His nose,
  His nose,
With a ring at the end of his nose.

"Dear Pig, are you willing to sell for one shilling
 Your ring?" Said the Piggy, "I will."
So they took it away, and were married next day
 By the Turkey who lives on the hill.
They dined on mince, and slices of quince,
 Which they ate with a runcible spoon;
And hand in hand, on the edge of the sand,
 They danced by the light of the moon,
  The moon,
  The moon,
They danced by the light of the moon.

Jabberwocky, by Lewis Carroll, 1832 – 98
(*From the first chapter of* Alice Through the Looking Glass)

'Twas brillig, and the slithy toves
   Did gyre and gimble in the wabe:
All mimsy were the borogoves,
   And the mome raths outgrabe.

"Beware the Jabberwock, my son!
   The jaws that bite, the claws that catch!
Beware the Jubjub bird, and shun
   The frumious Bandersnatch!"

He took his vorpal sword in hand;
   Long time the manxome foe he sought—
So rested he by the Tumtum tree
   And stood awhile in thought.

And, as in uffish thought he stood,
   The Jabberwock, with eyes of flame,
Came whiffling through the tulgey wood,
   And burbled as it came!

One, two! One, two! And through and through
   The vorpal blade went snicker-snack!
He left it dead, and with its head
   He went galumphing back.

"And hast thou slain the Jabberwock?
   Come to my arms, my beamish boy!
O frabjous day! Callooh! Callay!"
   He chortled in his joy.

'Twas brillig, and the slithy toves
   Did gyre and gimble in the wabe:
All mimsy were the borogoves,
   And the mome raths outgrabe.

Father William, by Lewis Carrol, 1832 – 98
(*From chapter 5 of* Alice in Wonderland)

"You are old, Father William," the young man said,
"And your hair has become very white;
And yet you incessantly stand on your head –
Do you think, at your age, it is right?"
"In my youth," Father William replied to his son,
"I feared it might injure the brain;
But, now that I'm perfectly sure I have none,
Why, I do it again and again."

"You are old," said the youth, "as I mentioned before,
And have grown most uncommonly fat;
Yet you turned a back-somersault in at the door –
Pray, what is the reason of that?"
"In my youth," said the sage, as he shook his grey locks,
"I kept all my limbs very supple
By the use of this ointment – one shilling the box –
Allow me to sell you a couple?"

"You are old," said the youth, "and your jaws are too weak
For anything tougher than suet;
Yet you finished the goose, with the bones and the beak –
Pray, how did you manage to do it?"
"In my youth," said his father, "I took to the law,
And argued each case with my wife;
And the muscular strength, which it gave to my jaw,
Has lasted the rest of my life."

"You are old," said the youth, "one would hardly suppose
That your eye was as steady as ever;
Yet you balanced an eel on the end of your nose –
What made you so awfully clever?"
"I have answered three questions, and that is enough,"
Said his father; "don't give yourself airs!
Do you think I can listen all day to such stuff?
Be off, or I'll kick you downstairs!"

Chard Whitlow (*Mr Eliot's Sunday Evening Postscript*), by Henry Reed, 1914 – 1986

As we get older we do not get any younger.
Seasons return, and to-day I am fifty-five,
And this time last year I was fifty-four
And this time next year I shall be sixty-two.
And I cannot say I should like (to speak for myself)
To see my time over again - if you can call it time:
Fidgeting uneasily under a draughty stair,
Or counting sleepless nights in the crowded tube.

There are certain precautions - though none of them very reliable -
Against the blast from bombs and the flying splinter,
But not against the blast from heaven, *vento dei venti*,
The wind within a wind unable to speak for wind;
And the frigid burnings of purgatory will not be touched
By any emollient.
        I think you will find this put,
Better than I could ever hope to express it,
In the words of Kharma: 'It is, we believe,
Idle to hope that the simple stirrup-pump
Will extinguish hell.'
        Oh, listeners,
And you especially who have turned off the wireless,
And sit in Stoke or Basingstoke listening appreciatively to the
    silence,
(Which is also the silence of hell) pray, not for your skins, but
    for your souls.

And pray for me also under the draughty stair.
As we get older we do not get any younger.

And pray for Kharma under the holy mountain.

Annus Mirabilis, by Philip Larkin, 1922 – 1985

Sexual intercourse began
In nineteen sixty-three
(which was rather late for me) -
Between the end of the Chatterley ban
And the Beatles' first LP.

Up to then there'd only been
A sort of bargaining,
A wrangle for the ring,
A shame that started at sixteen
And spread to everything.

Then all at once the quarrel sank:
Everyone felt the same,
And every life became
A brilliant breaking of the bank,
A quite unlosable game.

So life was never better than
In nineteen sixty-three
(Though just too late for me) -
Between the end of the Chatterley ban
And the Beatles' first LP.

This Be The Verse, by Philip Larkin, 1922 – 85

They fuck you up, your mum and dad.
 They may not mean to, but they do.
They fill you with the faults they had
 And add some extra, just for you.

But they were fucked up in their turn
 By fools in old-style hats and coats,
Who half the time were soppy-stern
 And half at one another's throats.

Man hands on misery to man.
 It deepens like a coastal shelf.
Get out as early as you can,
 And don't have any kids yourself.

Warning, by Jenny Joseph, born in 1932

When I am an old woman I shall wear purple
With a red hat which doesn't go, and doesn't suit me.
And I shall spend my pension on brandy and summer gloves
And satin sandals, and say we've no money for butter.
I shall sit down on the pavement when I'm tired
And gobble up samples in shops and press alarm bells
And run my stick along the public railings
And make up for the sobriety of my youth.
I shall go out in my slippers in the rain
And pick the flowers in other people's gardens
And learn to spit.

You can wear terrible shirts and grow more fat
And eat three pounds of sausages at a go
Or only bread and pickle for a week
And hoard pens and pencils and beermats and things in boxes.

But now we must have clothes that keep us dry
And pay our rent and not swear in the street
And set a good example for the children.
We must have friends to dinner and read the papers.

But maybe I ought to practice a little now?
So people who know me are not too shocked and surprised
When suddenly I am old, and start to wear purple.

How To Get On In Society, by John Betjeman, 1906 – 1984

Phone for the fish knives, Norman
As cook is a little unnerved;
You kiddies have crumpled the serviettes
And I must have things daintily served.

Are the requisites all in the toilet?
The frills round the cutlets can wait
Till the girl has replenished the cruets
And switched on the logs in the grate.

It's ever so close in the lounge dear,
But the vestibule's comfy for tea
And Howard is riding on horseback
So do come and take some with me.

Now here is a fork for your pastries
And do use the couch for your feet;
I know that I wanted to ask you-
Is trifle sufficient for sweet?

Milk and then just as it comes dear?
I'm afraid the preserve's full of stones;
Beg pardon, I'm soiling the doileys
With afternoon tea-cakes and scones.

Bloody Men, by Wendy Cope, born in 1945

Bloody men are like bloody buses -
You wait for about a year
And as soon as one approaches your stop
Two or three others appear.

You look at them flashing their indicators,
Offering you a ride.
You're trying to read the destinations,
You haven't much time to decide.

If you make a mistake, there is no turning back.
Jump off, and you'll stand there and gaze
While the cars and the taxis and lorries go by
And the minutes, the hours, the days.

Flowers, also by Wendy Cope

Some men never think of it.
You did. You'd come along
And say you'd nearly brought me flowers
But something had gone wrong.

The shop was closed. Or you had doubts –
The sort that minds like ours
Dream up incessantly. You thought
I might not want your flowers.

It made me smile and hug you then.
Now I can only smile.
But, look, the flowers you nearly brought
Have lasted all this while.

After the Lunch, by Wendy Cope, born in 1945

On Waterloo Bridge, where we said our goodbyes,
The weather conditions bring tears to my eyes.
I wipe them away with a black woolly glove
And try not to notice I've fallen in love.

On Waterloo Bridge I am trying to think:
This is nothing. You're high on the charm and the drink.
But the juke-box inside me is playing a song
That says something different. And when was it wrong?

On Waterloo Bridge with the wind in my hair
I am tempted to skip. *You're a fool.* I don't care.
The head does its best but the heart is the boss-
I admit it before I am halfway across.

Valentine, also by Wendy Cope

My heart has made its mind up
And I'm afraid it's you.
Whatever you've got lined up,
My heart has made its mind up
And if you can't be signed up
This year, next year will do.
My heart has made its mind up
And I'm afraid it's you.

My Funeral, by Wendy Cope, born in 1945

I hope I can trust you, friends, not to use our relationship
As an excuse for an unsolicited ego-trip.

I have seen enough of them at funerals and they make me cross.
At this one, though deceased, I aim to be the boss.

If you are asked to talk about me for five minutes, please do not
   go on for eight.
There is a strict timetable at the crematorium and nobody wants
   to be late.

If invited to read a poem, just read the bloody poem. If requested
To sing a song, just sing it, as suggested,

And don't say anything. Though I will not be there,
Glancing pointedly at my watch and fixing the speaker with a
   malevolent stare,

Remember that this was how I always reacted
When I felt that anybody's speech, sermon or poetry reading was
   becoming too protracted.

Yes, I was intolerant, and not always polite
And if there aren't many people at my funeral, it will serve
   me right.

Rowan Williams, the former Archbishop of Canterbury, has written that 'Wendy Cope is without doubt the wittiest of contemporary poets, and says a lot of extremely serious things'.

Section VII

15 Narrative Poems

Fifteen Narrative Poems

Page

1. Lord Ullin's Daughter by Thomas Campbell,
   1777 – 1844   88

2. Abou Ben Adhem by James Leigh Hunt, 1784 – 1859   90

3. Horatius by Lord Macaulay, 1800 - 1859   91

4. The Sicilian's Tale (Robert of Sicily), from *Tales
   of the Wayside Inn* by Henry Wadsworth Longfellow,
   1807 – 1882   99

5. Porphyria's Lover by Robert Browning, 1812 – 1889   106

6. The Walrus and the Carpenter, by Lewis Carroll,
   1832 – 1898   108

7. The Farmer's Bride by Charlotte Mew, 1869 – 1928   112

8. Henry King by Hilaire Belloc, 1870 – 1953   114

9. The Listeners by Walter de la Mare, 1873 – 1956   115

10. The Highwayman by Alfred Noyes, 1880 – 1968   117

11. The Lion and Albert by George Marriot Edgar,
    1880 – 1951   121

12. Journey of the Magi by T.S.Eliot, 1888 – 1965   124

13. The Parable of the Old Man and the Young
    by Wilfred Owen, 1893 – 1918   126

14. Original Sin on the Sussex Coast
    by John Betjeman, 1906 – 1984   127

15. Death in Leamington by John Betjeman, 1906 – 1984   128

Lord Ullin's Daughter by Thomas Campbell, 1777 – 1844

This is a poem which our mother read to my brother and me during the Blitz of 1940 – 41, when we were six and in our Anderson shelter in the garden.

A chieftain, to the Highlands bound,
Cries, "Boatman, do not tarry!
And I'll give thee a silver pound
To row us o'er the ferry!"

"Now, who be ye, would cross Lochgyle,
This dark and stormy water?"
"O, I'm the chief of Ulva's isle,
And this, Lord Ullin's daughter.

"And fast before her father's men
Three days we've fled together,
For should he find us in the glen,
My blood would stain the heather.

"His horsemen hard behind us ride;
Should they our steps discover,
Then who will cheer my bonny bride
When they have slain her lover?"

Out spoke the hardy Highland wight,
"I'll go, my chief, I'm ready:
It is not for your silver bright,
But for your winsome lady:-

"And by my word! the bonny bird
In danger shall not tarry;
So, though the waves are raging white,
I'll row you o'er the ferry."

By this the storm grew loud apace,
The water-wraith was shrieking;

And in the scowl of heaven each face
Grew dark as they were speaking.

But still as wilder blew the wind,
And as the night grew drearer,
Adown the glen rode armèd men,
Their trampling sounded nearer.

"O haste thee, haste!" the lady cries,
"Though tempests round us gather;
I'll meet the raging of the skies,
But not an angry father."

The boat has left a stormy land,
A stormy sea before her,–
When, O! too strong for human hand,
The tempest gather'd o'er her.

And still they row'd amidst the roar
Of waters fast prevailing:
Lord Ullin reach'd that fatal shore,-
His wrath was changed to wailing.

For, sore dismay'd, through storm and shade,
His child he did discover:-
One lovely hand she stretch'd for aid,
And one was round her lover.

"Come back! come back!" he cried in grief
"Across this stormy water:
And I'll forgive your Highland chief,
My daughter!- Oh, my daughter!"

'Twas vain: the loud waves lash'd the shore,
Return or aid preventing:
The waters wild went o'er his child,
And he was left lamenting.

Abhu Ben Adhem, by James Leigh Hunt, 1784 – 1859

James Leigh Hunt was educated at Christ's Hospital in the days when it was at Newgate Street in London. He was a few years younger than Coleridge and Lamb, who were also at school there and were near contemporaries.

Abhu Ben Adhem *is the best known of all Leigh Hunt's poems. It is the shortest in this group of fifteen narrative poems and is a model of economy.*

Abou Ben Adhem (may his tribe increase!)
Awoke one night from a deep dream of peace,
And saw, within the moonlight in his room,
Making it rich, and like a lily in bloom,
An angel writing in a book of gold:
Exceeding peace had made Ben Adhem bold,
And to the presence in the room he said,
"What writest thou?" The vision raised its head,
And with a look made of all sweet accord,
Answered, "The names of those who love the Lord."
"And is mine one?" said Abou. "Nay, not so,"
Replied the angel. Abou spoke more low,
But cheerly still, and said "I pray thee, then,
Write me as one that loves his fellow men."
The angel wrote, and vanished. The next night
It came again with a great wakening light,
And showed the names whom love of God had blessed,
And lo! Ben Adhem's name led all the rest.

Horatius, by Lord Macaulay, 1800 - 1859

*This is the version of Lord Macaulay's 'lay made about the year of the city CCCLX' which my younger son, Piers, on his own initiative, copied out meticulously in his best handwriting, fitting it neatly into an exercise book, during the couple of weeks after his seventh birthday on 1*st *July 1972, in time to give to his mother on her 37*th *birthday on 16*th *July.*

Macaulay makes the assumption that the reader will know the story of the rape of Lucretia by Sextus Tarquinius, the son of the last king of Rome, Tarquin the Proud, and how this resulted in the establishment of the Roman Republic. His poem, which has seventy stanzas, tells the story of what happened after Sextus Tarquinius appealed for help to a neighbouring ruler, Lars Porsena of Clusium, one of the cities of Etruria, then dominant in the Italian peninsula and to the north of Rome.

The Janiculum (stanza 19) is a tall hill west of the River Tiber, outside the boundaries of the ancient city, and commanding the western approaches to Rome.

Mount Algidus (stanza 68) was a wooded area to the south-east of Rome.

This version has only twenty-one stanzas, but it tells the story nonetheless. The numbering of the stanzas makes clear which have been omitted in this version. Numbers 3 -12 are largely about the preparations for defence. Numbers 39 – 48 tell how one after another the Etruscan champions were slain by Horatius and his comrades.

1. Lars Porsena of Clusium
By the Nine Gods he swore
That the great house of Tarquin
Should suffer wrong no more.
By the Nine Gods he swore it,
And named a trysting day,
And bade his messengers ride forth,
East and west and south and north,
To summon his array.

2. East and west and south and north
The messengers ride fast,
And tower and town and cottage
Have heard the trumpet's blast.
Shame on the false Etruscan
Who lingers in his home,
When Porsena of Clusium
Is on the march for Rome.

13. But by the yellow Tiber
Was tumult and affright:
From all the spacious champaign
To Rome men took their flight.
A mile around the city,
The throng stopped up the ways;
A fearful sight it was to see
Through two long nights and days.

19. They held a council standing
Before the River-Gate;
Short time was there, ye well may guess,
For musing or debate.
Out spake the Consul roundly:
'The bridge must straight go down;
For, since Janiculum is lost,
Naught else can save the town.'

27. Then out spake brave Horatius,
The Captain of the Gate:
'To every man upon this earth
Death cometh soon or late.
And how can man die better
Than facing fearful odds,
For the ashes of his fathers,
And the temples of his gods?'

29. 'Hew down the bridge, Sir Consul,
With all the speed ye may;
I, with two more to help me,
Will hold the foe in play.
In yon strait path a thousand
May well be stopped by three.
Now who will stand on either hand,
And keep the bridge with me?'

30. Then out spake Spurius Lartius;
A Ramnian proud was he:
'Lo, I will stand at thy right hand,
And keep the bridge with thee.'
And out spake strong Herminius;
Of Titian blood was he:
'I will abide on thy left side,
And keep the bridge with thee.'

36. The Three stood calm and silent
And looked upon the foes,
And a great shout of laughter
From all the vanguard rose:
And forth three chiefs came spurring
Before that deep array;
To earth they sprang, their swords they drew,
And lifted high their shields, and flew
To win the narrow way.

38. Stout Lartius hurled down Aunus
Into the stream beneath;
Herminius struck at Seius,
And clove him to the teeth;
At Picus brave Horatius
Darted one fiery thrust;
And the proud Umbrian's gilded arms
Clashed in the bloody dust.

49. But all Etruria's noblest
Felt their hearts sink to see
On the earth the bloody corpses,
In the path the dauntless Three:
And, from the ghastly entrance
Where those bold Romans stood,
All shrank, like boys who unaware,
Ranging the woods to start a hare,
Come to the mouth of the dark lair
Where, growling low, a fierce old bear
Lies amidst bones and blood.

50. Was none who would be foremost
To lead such dire attack;
But those behind cried, 'Forward!'
And those before cried, 'Back!'
And backward now and forward
Wavers the deep array;
And on the tossing sea of steel
To and frow the standards reel;
And the victorious trumpet-peal
Dies fitfully away.

53. But meanwhile axe and lever
Have manfully been plied;
And now the bridge hangs tottering
Above the boiling tide.
'Come back, come back, Horatius!'
Loud cried the Fathers all.
'Back, Lartius! back, Herminius!
Back, ere the ruin fall!'

54. Back darted Spurius Lartius;
Herminius darted back:
And, as they passed, beneath their feet
They felt the timbers crack.
But when they turned their faces,
And on the farther shore
Saw brave Horatius stand alone,
They would have crossed once more.

57. Alone stood brave Horatius,
But constant still in mind;
Thrice thirty thousand foes before,
And the broad flood behind.
'Down with him!' cried false Sextus,
With a smile on his pale face.
'Now yield thee,' cried Lars Porsena,
'Now yield thee to our grace.'

58. Round turned he, as not deigning
Those craven ranks to see;
Nought spake he to Lars Porsena,
To Sextus nought spake he;
But he saw on Palatinus
The white porch of his home;
And he spake to the noble river
That rolls by the towers of Rome.

59. 'Oh, Tiber! Father Tiber!
To whom the Romans pray,
A Roman's life, a Roman's arms,
Take thou in charge this day!'
So he spake, and speaking sheathed
The good sword by his side,
And with his harness on his back,
Plunged headlong in the tide.

60. No sound of joy or sorrow
Was heard from either bank;
But friends and foes in dumb surprise,
With parted lips and straining eyes,
Stood gazing where he sank;
And when above the surges,
They saw his crest appear,
All Rome sent forth a rapturous cry,
And even the ranks of Tuscany
Could scarce forbear to cheer.

62. Never, I ween, did swimmer,
In such an evil case,
Struggle through such a raging flood
Safe to the landing place:
But his limbs were borne up bravely
By the brave heart within,
And our good father Tiber
Bare bravely up his chin.

64. And now he feels the bottom;
Now on dry earth he stands;
Now round him throng the Fathers
To press his gory hands;
And now, with shouts and clapping,
And noise of weeping loud,
He enters through the River-Gate
Borne by the joyous crowd.

68. And in the nights of winter,
When the cold north winds blow,
And the long howling of the wolves
Is heard amidst the snow;
When round the lonely cottage
Roars loud the tempest's din,
And the good logs of Algidus
Roar louder yet within;

70. When the goodman mends his armour,
And trims his helmet's plume;
When the goodwife's shuttle merrily
Goes flashing through the loom;
With weeping and with laughter
Still is the story told,
How well Horatius kept the bridge
In the brave days of old.

The Sicilian's Tale, ('Robert of Sicily', from *Tales of a Wayside Inn*), by Henry Wadsworth Longfellow, 1807 – 84.

Robert of Sicily, brother of Pope Urbane
And Valmond, Emperor of Allemaine,
Apparelled in magnificent attire,
With retinue of many a knight and squire,
On St. John's eve, at vespers, proudly sat
And heard the priests chant the Magnificat,
And as he listened, o'er and o'er again
Repeated, like a burden or refrain,
He caught the words, "Deposuit potentes
De sede, et exaltavit humiles;"
And slowly lifting up his kingly head
He to a learned clerk beside him said,
"What mean these words?" The clerk made answer meet,
"He has put down the mighty from their seat,
And has exalted them of low degree."
Thereat King Robert muttered scornfully,
"'Tis well that such seditious words are sung
Only by priests and in the Latin tongue;
For unto priests and people be it known,
There is no power can push me from my throne!"
And leaning back, he yawned and fell asleep,
Lulled by the chant monotonous and deep.

When he awoke, it was already night;
The church was empty, and there was no light,
Save where the lamps, that glimmered few and faint,
Lighted a little space before some saint.
He started from his seat and gazed around,
But saw no living thing and heard no sound.
He groped towards the door, but it was locked;
He cried aloud, and listened, and then knocked,
And uttered awful threatenings and complaints,
And imprecations upon men and saints.

The sounds reëchoed from the roof and walls
As if dead priests were laughing in their stalls.

At length the sexton, hearing from without
The tumult of the knocking and the shout,
And thinking thieves were in the house of prayer,
Came with his lantern, asking, "Who is there?"
Half choked with rage, King Robert fiercely said,
"Open: 'tis I, the King! Art thou afraid?"
The frightened sexton, muttering, with a curse,
"This is some drunken vagabond, or worse!"
Turned the great key and flung the portal wide;
A man rushed by him at a single stride,
Haggard, half naked, without hat or cloak,
Who neither turned, nor looked at him, nor spoke,
But leaped into the blackness of the night,
And vanished like a spectre from his sight.

Robert of Sicily, brother of Pope Urbane
And Valmond, Emperor of Allemaine,
Despoiled of his magnificent attire,
Bareheaded, breathless, and besprent with mire,
With sense of wrong and outrage desperate,
Strode on and thundered at the palace gate;
Rushed through the courtyard, thrusting in his rage
To right and left each seneschal and page,
And hurried up the broad and sounding stair,
His white face ghastly in the torches' glare.
From hall to hall he passed with breathless speed;
Voices and cries he heard, but did not heed,
Until at last he reached the banquet-room,
Blazing with light, and breathing with perfume.

There on the dais sat another king,
Wearing his robes, his crown, his signet-ring,
King Robert's self in features, form, and height,
But all transfigured with angelic light!

It was an Angel; and his presence there
With a divine effulgence filled the air,
An exaltation, piercing the disguise,
Though none the hidden Angel recognize.

A moment speechless, motionless, amazed,
The throneless monarch on the Angel gazed,
Who met his look of anger and surprise
With the divine compassion of his eyes;
Then said, "Who art thou? and why com'st thou here?"
To which King Robert answered, with a sneer,
"I am the King, and come to claim my own
From an impostor, who usurps my throne!"
And suddenly, at these audacious words,
Up sprang the angry guests, and drew their swords;

The Angel answered, with unruffled brow,
"Nay, not the King, but the King's Jester, thou
Henceforth shalt wear the bells and scalloped cape,
And for thy counsellor shalt lead an ape;
Thou shalt obey my servants when they call,
And wait upon my henchmen in the hall!"

Deaf to King Robert's threats and cries and prayers,
They thrust him from the hall and down the stairs;
A group of tittering pages ran before,
And as they opened wide the folding-door,
His heart failed, for he heard, with strange alarms,
The boisterous laughter of the men-at-arms,
And all the vaulted chamber roar and ring
With the mock plaudits of "Long live the King!"

Next morning, waking with the day's first beam,
He said within himself, "It was a dream!"
But the straw rustled as he turned his head,
There were the cap and bells beside his bed,
Around him rose the bare, discolored walls,
Close by, the steeds were champing in their stalls,

And in the corner, a revolting shape,
Shivering and chattering sat the wretched ape.
It was no dream; the world he loved so much
Had turned to dust and ashes at his touch!

Days came and went; and now returned again
To Sicily the old Saturnian reign;
Under the Angel's governance benign
The happy island danced with corn and wine,
And deep within the mountain's burning breast
Enceladus, the giant, was at rest.

Meanwhile King Robert yielded to his fate,
Sullen and silent and disconsolate.
Dressed in the motley garb that Jesters wear,
With look bewildered and a vacant stare,
Close shaven above the ears, as monks are shorn,
By courtiers mocked, by pages laughed to scorn,
His only friend the ape, his only food
What others left, - he still was unsubdued.
And when the Angel met him on his way,
And half in earnest, half in jest, would say,
Sternly, though tenderly, that he might feel
The velvet scabbard held a sword of steel,
"Art thou the King?" the passion of his woe
Burst from him in resistless overflow,
And, lifting high his forehead, he would fling
The haughty answer back, "I am, I am the King!"

Almost three years were ended; when there came
Ambassadors of great repute and name
From Valmond, Emperor of Allemaine,
Unto King Robert, saying that Pope Urbane
By letter summoned them forthwith to come
On Holy Thursday to his city of Rome.
The Angel with great joy received his guests,
And gave them presents of embroidered vests,
And velvet mantles with rich ermine lined,

And rings and jewels of the rarest kind.
Then he departed with them o'er the sea
Into the lovely land of Italy,
Whose loveliness was more resplendent made
By the mere passing of that cavalcade,
With plumes, and cloaks, and housings, and the stir
Of jewelled bridle and of golden spur.
And lo! among the menials, in mock state,
Upon a piebald steed, with shambling gait,
His cloak of fox-tails flapping in the wind,
The solemn ape demurely perched behind,
King Robert rode, making huge merriment
In all the country towns through which they went.

The Pope received them with great pomp and blare
Of bannered trumpets, on Saint Peter's square,
Giving his benediction and embrace,
Fervent, and full of apostolic grace,
While with congratulations and with prayers
He entertained the Angel unawares.
Robert, the Jester, bursting through the crowd,
Into their presence rushed, and cried aloud,
"I am the King! Look, and behold in me
Robert, your brother, King of Sicily!
This man, who wears my semblance to your eyes,
Is an impostor in a king's disguise.
Do you not know me? does no voice within
Answer my cry, and say we are akin?"
The Pope in silence, but with troubled mien,
Gazed at the Angel's countenance serene;
The Emperor, laughing, said, "It is strange sport
To keep a madman for thy Fool at court!"
And the poor, baffled Jester in disgrace
Was hustled back among the populace.

In solemn state the Holy Week went by,
And Easter Sunday gleamed upon the sky;

The presence of the Angel, with its light,
Before the sun rose, made the city bright,
And with new fervor filled the hearts of men,
Who felt that Christ indeed had risen again.
Even the Jester, on his bed of straw,
With haggard eyes the unwonted splendor saw,
He felt within a power unfelt before,
And, kneeling humbly on his chamber floor,
He heard the rushing garments of the Lord
Sweep through the silent air, ascending heavenward.

And now the visit ending, and once more
Valmond returning to the Danube's shore,
Homeward the Angel journeyed, and again
The land was made resplendent with his train,
Flashing along the towns of Italy
Unto Salerno, and from thence by sea.
And when once more within Palermo's wall,
And, seated on the throne in his great hall,
He heard the Angelus from convent towers,
As if the better world conversed with ours,
He beckoned to King Robert to draw nigher,
And with a gesture bade the rest retire;
And when they were alone, the Angel said,
"Art thou the King?" Then, bowing down his head,
King Robert crossed both hands upon his breast,
And meekly answered him: "Thou knowest best!
My sins as scarlet are; let me go hence,
And in some cloister's school of penitence,
Across those stones, that pave the way to heaven,
Walk barefoot, till my guilty soul be shriven!"

The Angel smiled, and from his radiant face
A holy light illumined all the place,
And through the open window, loud and clear,
They heard the monks chant in the chapel near,
Above the stir and tumult of the street:

"He has put down the mighty from their seat,
And has exalted them of low degree!"
And through the chant a second melody
Rose like the throbbing of a single string:
"I am an Angel, and thou art the King!"

King Robert, who was standing near the throne,
Lifted his eyes, and lo! He was alone!
But all apparelled as in days of old,
With ermined mantle and with cloth of gold;
And when his courtiers came, they found him there
Kneeling upon the floor, absorbed in silent prayer.

Porphyria's Lover, by Robert Browning, 1812 – 89

The rain set early in to-night,
   The sullen wind was soon awake,
It tore the elm-tops down for spite,
   And did its worst to vex the lake:
   I listened with heart fit to break.

When glided in Porphyria; straight
   She shut the cold out and the storm,
And kneeled and made the cheerless grate
   Blaze up, and all the cottage warm;
   Which done, she rose, and from her form

Withdrew the dripping cloak and shawl,
   And laid her soiled gloves by, untied
Her hat and let the damp hair fall,
   And, last, she sat down by my side
   And called me. When no voice replied,

She put my arm about her waist,
   And made her smooth white shoulder bare,
And all her yellow hair displaced,
   And, stooping, made my cheek lie there,
   And spread, o'er all, her yellow hair,

Murmuring how she loved me — she
   Too weak, for all her heart's endeavour,
To set its struggling passion free
   From pride, and vainer ties dissever,
   And give herself to me for ever.

But passion sometimes would prevail,
   Nor could to-night's gay feast restrain
A sudden thought of one so pale
   For love of her, and all in vain:
   So, she was come through wind and rain.

Be sure I looked up at her eyes
   Happy and proud; at last I knew
Porphyria worshipped me; surprise
   Made my heart swell, and still it grew
   While I debated what to do.

That moment she was mine, mine, fair,
   Perfectly pure and good: I found
A thing to do, and all her hair
   In one long yellow string I wound
   Three times her little throat around,

And strangled her. No pain felt she;
   I am quite sure she felt no pain.
As a shut bud that holds a bee,
   I warily oped her lids: again
   Laughed the blue eyes without a stain.

And I untightened next the tress
   About her neck; her cheek once more
Blushed bright beneath my burning kiss:
   I propped her head up as before,
   Only, this time my shoulder bore

Her head, which droops upon it still:
   The smiling rosy little head,
So glad it has its utmost will,
   That all it scorned at once is fled,
   And I, its love, am gained instead!

Porphyria's love: she guessed not how
   Her darling one wish would be heard.
And thus we sit together now,
   And all night long we have not stirred,
   And yet God has not said a word!

The Walrus and the Carpenter, by Lewis Carroll, 1832 – 98
(A story told to Alice by Tweedledee in
chapter IV of **Through the Looking Glass***)*

The sun was shining on the sea,
  Shining with all his might:
He did his very best to make
  The billows smooth and bright —
And this was odd, because it was
  The middle of the night.

The moon was shining sulkily,
  Because she thought the sun
Had got no business to be there
  After the day was done —
"It's very rude of him," she said,
  "To come and spoil the fun."

The sea was wet as wet could be,
  The sands were dry as dry.
You could not see a cloud, because
  No cloud was in the sky:
No birds were flying overhead —
  There were no birds to fly.

The Walrus and the Carpenter
  Were walking close at hand;
They wept like anything to see
  Such quantities of sand:
'If this were only cleared away,'
  They said, 'it would be grand!'

'If seven maids with seven mops
  Swept it for half a year,
Do you suppose,' the Walrus said,
  'That they could get it clear?'
'I doubt it,' said the Carpenter,
  And shed a bitter tear.

'O Oysters, come and walk with us!'
  The Walrus did beseech.
'A pleasant walk, a pleasant talk,
  Along the briny beach:
'We cannot do with more than four,
  To give a hand to each.'

The eldest Oyster looked at him,
  But never a word he said:
The eldest Oyster winked his eye,
  And shook his heavy head —
Meaning to say he did not choose
  To leave the oyster-bed.

But four young Oysters hurried up,
  All eager for the treat:
Their coats were brushed, their faces washed,
  Their shoes were clean and neat -
And this was odd, because, you know,
  They hadn't any feet.

Four other Oysters followed them,
  And yet another four;
And thick and fast they came at last,
  And more, and more, and more —
All hopping through the frothy waves,
  And scrambling to the shore.

The Walrus and the Carpenter
  Walked on a mile or so,
And then they rested on a rock
  Conveniently low:
And all the little Oysters stood
  And waited in a row.

'The time has come,' the Walrus said,
  'To talk of many things:
Of shoes — and ships — and sealing-wax —
  Of cabbages — and kings —
And why the sea is boiling hot —
  And whether pigs have wings.'

'But wait a bit,' the Oysters cried,
  'Before we have our chat;
For some of us are out of breath,
  And all of us are fat!'
'No hurry!' said the Carpenter.
  They thanked him much for that.

'A loaf of bread,' the Walrus said,
  'Is what we chiefly need:
Pepper and vinegar besides
  Are very good indeed —
Now if you're ready, Oysters dear,
  We can begin to feed.'

'But not on us!' the Oysters cried,
  Turning a little blue.
'After such kindness, that would be
  A dismal thing to do!'
'The night is fine,' the Walrus said.
  'Do you admire the view?

It was so kind of you to come!
  And you are very nice!'
The Carpenter said nothing but
  'Cut us another slice -
I wish you were not quite so deaf –
  I've had to ask you twice!'

'It seems a shame,' the Walrus said,
  'To play them such a trick,
After we've brought them out so far,
  And made them trot so quick!'
The Carpenter said nothing but
  'The butter's spread too thick!'

'I weep for you,' the Walrus said:
  'I deeply sympathize.'
With sobs and tears he sorted out
  Those of the largest size,
Holding his pocket-handkerchief
  Before his streaming eyes.

'O Oysters,' said the Carpenter,
  'You've had a pleasant run!
Shall we be trotting home again?'
  But answer came there none —
And this was scarcely odd, because
  They'd eaten every one.

The Farmer's Bride, by Charlotte Mew, 1869 – 1928

*Charlotte Mew was one of seven siblings, four boys
and three girls. Three of her brothers died young. The other
one was committed to a psychiatric hospital, then known as a
lunatic asylum, as was one of her sisters. After the other sister
died of cancer in 1927, she became seriously depressed and
committed suicide the following year.*

Three summers since I chose a maid,
Too young maybe—but more's to do
At harvest-time than bide and woo.
     When us was wed she turned afraid
     Of love and me and all things human;
     Like the shut of a winter's day
     Her smile went out, and 'twadn't a woman—
        More like a little frightened fay.
        One night, in the Fall, she runned away.

"Out 'mong the sheep, her be," they said,
"Should properly have been abed;"
But sure enough she wadn't there
Lying awake with her wide brown stare.
So over seven-acre field and up-along across the
    down
We chased her, flying like a hare
Before out lanterns to Church-Town.
     All in a shiver and a scare
We caught her, fetched her home at last
     And turned the key upon her, fast.

She does the work about the house
    As well as must, but like a mouse:
        Happy enough to chat and play
        With birds and rabbits and such as they,
        So long as men-folk keep away.
"Not near, not near!" her eyes beseech
When one of us comes within reach.

The woman say that beasts in stall
Look round like children at her call.
I've hardly heard her speak at all.

Shy as a leveret, swift as he,
Straight and slight as a young larch tree,
Sweet as the first wild violets, she,
To her wild self. But what to me?

The short days shorten and the oaks are brown,
    The blue smoke rises to the low grey sky,
One leaf in the still air falls slowly down,
    A magpie's spotted feathers lie
On the black earth spread white with rime,
The berries redden up to Christmas-time.
    What's Christmas-time without there be
    Some other in the house than we!

    She sleeps up in the attic there
    Alone, poor maid. 'Tis but a stair
Betwixt us. Oh! my God! the down,
    The soft young down of her, the brown,
The brown of her—her eyes, her hair, her hair!

Henry King, who ate string and was cut off in dreadful agonies, by Hilaire Belloc, 1870 – 1953

The Chief Defect of Henry King
Was chewing little bits of String.

At last he swallowed some which tied
Itself in ugly Knots inside.

Physicians of the Utmost Fame
Were called at once; but when they came

They answered, as they took their Fees,
'There is no Cure for this Disease.

Henry will very soon be dead.'
His parents stood about his Bed

Lamenting his Untimely Death,
When Henry, with his Latest Breath,

Cried 'Oh, my Friends, be warned by me,
That Breakfast, Dinner, Lunch, and Tea

Are all the Human Frame requires...'
With that, the Wretched Child expires.

The Listeners by Walter De La Mare, 1873 – 1956

*This is a narrative poem in which almost nothing happens and we
are left to wonder why. Therein lies its power. It is also different
from most English poetry in that it does not have a regular metre
or rhythm. Instead there are three stresses to each line, and that
contributes to the feeling of strangeness.*

'Is there anybody there?' said the Traveller,
  Knocking on the moonlit door;
And his horse in the silence champed the grasses
  Of the forest's ferny floor:

And a bird flew up out of the turret,
  Above the Traveller's head:
And he smote upon the door again a second time;
  'Is there anybody there?' he said.

But no one descended to the Traveller;
  No head from the leaf-fringed sill
Leaned over and looked into his grey eyes,
  Where he stood perplexed and still.

But only a host of phantom listeners
  That dwelt in the lone house then
Stood listening in the quiet of the moonlight
  To that voice from the world of men:

Stood thronging the faint moonbeams on the dark stair,
  That goes down to the empty hall,
Hearkening in an air stirred and shaken
  By the lonely Traveller's call.

And he felt in his heart their strangeness,
  Their stillness answering his cry,
While his horse moved, cropping the dark turf,
  'Neath the starred and leafy sky;

For he suddenly smote on the door, even
  Louder, and lifted his head:—
'Tell them I came, and no one answered,
  That I kept my word,' he said.

Never the least stir made the listeners,
  Though every word he spake
Fell echoing through the shadowiness of the still house
  From the one man left awake:

Ay, they heard his foot upon the stirrup,
  And the sound of iron on stone,
And how the silence surged softly backward,
  When the plunging hoofs were gone.

Walter de la Mare was a prolific writer, particularly of novels, short stories and poetry. The Listeners *is now the poem by which he is best remembered.*

The Highwayman, by Alfred Noyes, 1880 – 1968

Part one

The wind was a torrent of darkness among the gusty trees,
The moon was a ghostly galleon tossed upon cloudy seas,
The road was a ribbon of moonlight over the purple moor,
And the highwayman came riding—
Riding—riding—
The highwayman came riding, up to the old inn-door.

He'd a French cocked-hat on his forehead, a bunch of lace
    at his chin,
A coat of the claret velvet, and breeches of brown doe-skin;
They fitted with never a wrinkle: his boots were up to the thigh!
And he rode with a jewelled twinkle,
His pistol butts a-twinkle,
His rapier hilt a-twinkle, under the jewelled sky.

Over the cobbles he clattered and clashed in the dark inn-yard,
And he tapped with his whip on the shutters, but all was locked
    and barred;
He whistled a tune to the window, and who should be waiting
    there
But the landlord's black-eyed daughter,
Bess, the landlord's daughter,
Plaiting a dark red love-knot into her long black hair.

And dark in the dark old inn-yard a stable-wicket creaked
Where Tim the ostler listened; his face was white and peaked;
His eyes were hollows of madness, his hair like mouldy hay,
But he loved the landlord's daughter,
The landlord's red-lipped daughter,
Dumb as a dog he listened, and he heard the robber say—

'One kiss, my bonny sweetheart, I'm after a prize to-night,
But I shall be back with the yellow gold before the morning
    light;

Yet, if they press me sharply, and harry me through the day,
Then look for me by moonlight,
Watch for me by moonlight,
I'll come to thee by moonlight, though hell should bar the way.'

He rose upright in the stirrups; he scarce could reach her hand,
But she loosened her hair i' the casement! His face burnt like
    a brand
As the black cascade of perfume came tumbling over his breast;
And he kissed its waves in the moonlight,
(Oh, sweet, black waves in the moonlight!)
Then he tugged at his rein in the moonlight, and galloped away
    to the West.

Part two
He did not come in the dawning; he did not come at noon;
And out o' the tawny sunset, before the rise o' the moon,
When the road was a gypsy's ribbon, looping the purple moor,
A red-coat troop came marching—
Marching—marching—
King George's men came marching, up to the old inn-door.

They said no word to the landlord, they drank his ale instead,
But they gagged his daughter and bound her to the foot of her
    narrow bed;
Two of them knelt at her casement, with muskets at their side!
There was death at every window;
And hell at one dark window;
For Bess could see, through her casement, the road that he
    would ride.

They had tied her up to attention, with many a sniggering jest;
They had bound a musket beside her, with the barrel beneath her
    breast!
'Now, keep good watch!' and they kissed her.
She heard the dead man say—
Look for me by moonlight;

Watch for me by moonlight;
I'll come to thee by moonlight, though hell should bar the way!

She twisted her hands behind her; but all the knots held good!
She writhed her hands till her fingers were wet with sweat or blood!
They stretched and strained in the darkness, and the hours
    crawled by like years,
Till, now, on the stroke of midnight,
Cold, on the stroke of midnight,
The tip of one finger touched it! The trigger at least was hers!

The tip of one finger touched it; she strove no more for the rest!
Up, she stood up to attention, with the barrel beneath her breast,
She would not risk their hearing; she would not strive again;
For the road lay bare in the moonlight;
Blank and bare in the moonlight;
And the blood of her veins in the moonlight throbbed to her
    love's refrain .

Tlot-tlot; tlot-tlot! Had they heard it? The horse-hoofs ringing
    clear;
Tlot-tlot, tlot-tlot, in the distance? Were they deaf that they did
    not hear?
Down the ribbon of moonlight, over the brow of the hill,
The highwayman came riding—
Riding—riding—
The red-coats looked to their priming! She stood up, straight and
    still!

Tlot-tlot, in the frosty silence! Tlot-tlot, in the echoing night!
Nearer he came and nearer! Her face was like a light!
Her eyes grew wide for a moment; she drew one last deep
    breath,
Then her finger moved in the moonlight,
Her musket shattered the moonlight,
Shattered her breast in the moonlight and warned him—with her
    death.

He turned; he spurred to the West; he did not know who stood
Bowed, with her head o'er the musket, drenched with her own
    red blood!
Not till the dawn he heard it, his face grew grey to hear
How Bess, the landlord's daughter,
The landlord's black-eyed daughter,
Had watched for her love in the moonlight, and died in the
    darkness there.

Back, he spurred like a madman, shrieking a curse to the sky,
With the white road smoking behind him and his rapier
    brandished high!
Blood-red were his spurs i' the golden noon; wine-red was his
    velvet coat,
When they shot him down on the highway,
Down like a dog on the highway,
And he lay in his blood on the highway, with the bunch of lace at
    his throat.

*And still of a winter's night, they say, when the wind is in the
    trees,*
When the moon is a ghostly galleon tossed upon cloudy seas,
When the road is a ribbon of moonlight over the purple moor,
A highwayman comes riding—
Riding—riding—
A highwayman comes riding, up to the old inn-door.

Over the cobbles he clatters and clangs in the dark inn-yard
*And he taps with his whip on the shutters, but all is locked
    and barred;*
*He whistles a tune to the window, and who should be
    waiting there*
But the landlord's black-eyed daughter,
Bess, the landlord's daughter,
Plaiting a dark red love-knot into her long black hair.

The Lion and Albert, by George Marriott Edgar, 1880 – 1951

This is the one poem in this collection which at one time could have been heard recited on stage in a Music Hall, particularly in Blackpool. It was a popular part of the repertoire of Stanley Holloway, 1890 – 1982. The third word in the last line may not always have been spoken as printed.

There's a famous seaside place called Blackpool,
That's noted for fresh air and fun,
And Mr and Mrs Ramsbottom
Went there with young Albert, their son.

A grand little lad was young Albert,
All dressed in his best; quite a swell
With a stick with an 'orse's 'ead 'andle,
The finest that Woolworth's could sell.

They didn't think much of the Ocean:
The waves, they were fiddlin' and small,
There was no wrecks and nobody drownded,
Fact, nothing to laugh at at all.

So, seeking for further amusement,
They paid and went into the Zoo,
Where they'd Lions and Tigers and Camels,
And old ale and sandwiches too.

There were one great big Lion called Wallace;
His nose were all covered with scars -
He lay in a somnolent posture,
With the side of his face on the bars.

Now Albert had heard about Lions,
How they was ferocious and wild -
To see Wallace lying so peaceful,
Well, it didn't seem right to the child.

So straightway the brave little feller,
Not showing a morsel of fear,
Took his stick with its 'orse's 'ead 'andle
And pushed it in Wallace's ear.

You could see that the Lion didn't like it,
For giving a kind of a roll,
He pulled Albert inside the cage with 'im,
And swallowed the little lad 'ole.

Then Pa, who had seen the occurrence,
And didn't know what to do next,
Said 'Mother! Yon Lion's 'et Albert',
And Mother said 'Well, I am vexed!'

Then Mr and Mrs Ramsbottom -
Quite rightly, when all's said and done -
Complained to the Animal Keeper,
That the Lion had eaten their son.

The keeper was quite nice about it;
He said 'What a nasty mishap.
Are you sure that it's your boy he's eaten?'
Pa said "Am I sure? There's his cap!'

The manager had to be sent for.
He came and he said 'What's to do?'
Pa said 'Yon Lion's 'et Albert,
'And 'im in his Sunday clothes, too.'

Then Mother said, 'Right's right, young feller;
I think it's a shame and a sin,
For a lion to go and eat Albert,
And after we've paid to come in.'

The manager wanted no trouble,
He took out his purse right away,
Saying 'How much to settle the matter?'
And Pa said "What do you usually pay?'

But Mother had turned a bit awkward
When she thought where her Albert had gone.
She said 'No! someone's got to be summonsed' -
So that was decided upon.

Then off they went to the P'lice Station,
In front of the Magistrate chap;
They told 'im what happened to Albert,
And proved it by showing his cap.

The Magistrate gave his opinion
That no one was really to blame
And he said that he hoped the Ramsbottoms
Would have further sons to their name.

At that Mother got proper blazing,
'And thank you, sir, kindly,' said she.
'What waste all our lives raising children
To feed ruddy Lions? Not me!'

Journey of the Magi, by T.S.Eliot, 1888 – 1965

*The first five lines of this poem are a quotation from a sermon
preached by Bishop Lancelot Andrewes at the court of King
James I at the Feast of the Epiphany, which celebrates the
coming of the Three Wise Men, or the Magi, to see the new-
born baby Jesus.*

'A cold coming we had of it,
Just the worst time of the year
For a journey, and such a long journey:
The ways deep and the weather sharp,
The very dead of winter.'
And the camels galled, sorefooted, refractory,
Lying down in the melting snow.
There were times we regretted
The summer palaces on slopes, the terraces,
And the silken girls bringing sherbet.

Then the camel men cursing and grumbling
And running away, and wanting their liquor and women,
And the night-fires going out, and the lack of shelters,
And the cities hostile and the towns unfriendly
And the villages dirty and charging high prices:
A hard time we had of it.
At the end we preferred to travel all night,
Sleeping in snatches,
With the voices singing in our ears, saying
That this was all folly.

Then at dawn we came down to a temperate valley,
Wet, below the snow line, smelling of vegetation,
With a running stream and a water-mill beating the
    darkness,
And three trees on the low sky,
And an old white horse galloped away in the meadow.
Then we came to a tavern with vine-leaves over the lintel,
Six hands at an open door dicing for pieces of silver,
And feet kicking the empty wine-skins.
But there was no information, and so we continued
And arrived at evening, not a moment too soon
Finding the place; it was (you might say) satisfactory.

All this was a long time ago, I remember,
And I would do it again, but set down
This set down
This: were we led all that way for
Birth or Death? There was a Birth, certainly,
We had evidence and no doubt. I had seen birth and death,
But had thought they were different; this Birth was
Hard and bitter agony for us, like Death, our death.
We returned to our places, these Kingdoms,
But no longer at ease here, in the old dispensation,
With an alien people clutching their gods.
I should be glad of another death.

The Parable of the Old Man and the Young,
by Wilfred Owen, 1893 – 1918

When Wilfred Owen wrote this poem, during the First World War, he could reasonably assume that anyone likely to read it would have known the story in chapter 22 of the Book of Genesis of how Abraham prepared to sacrifice his only son, Isaac, but was prevented from doing so by an angel calling him out of heaven, getting him to offer a ram instead.

More than half of the words in the poem come straight out of the King James Version of the Bible published in 1611. The force of the poem depends on knowing the original story and how it ends.

So Abram rose, and clave the wood, and went,
And took the fire with him, and a knife.
And as they sojourned both of them together,
Isaac the first-born spake and said, My Father,
Behold the preparations, fire and iron,
But where the lamb for this burnt-offering?
Then Abram bound the youth with belts and straps,
And builded parapets and trenches there,
And stretchèd forth the knife to slay his son.
When lo! an angel called him out of heaven,
Saying, Lay not thy hand upon the lad,
Neither do anything to him. Behold,
A ram, caught in a thicket by its horns;
Offer the Ram of Pride instead of him.
But the old man would not so, but slew his son,
And half the seed of Europe, one by one.

Original Sin on the Sussex Coast,
by John Betjeman, 1906 – 84

Now on this out of season afternoon
Day schools which cater for the sort of boy
Whose parents go by Pullman once a month
To do a show in town, pour out their young
Into the sharply red October light.
Here where The Drive and Buckhurst Road converge
I watch the rival gangs and am myself
A schoolboy once again in shivering shorts.
I see the dust of sherbet on the chin
Of Andrew Knox well-dress'd, well-born, well-fed,
Even at nine a perfect gentleman,
Willie Buchanan waiting at his side–
Another Scot, eruptions on his skin.
I hear Jack Drayton whistling from the fence
Which hides the copper domes of "Cooch Behar."
That was the signal. So there's no escape.
A race for Willow Way and jump the hedge
Behind the Granville Bowling Club? Too late.
They'll catch me coming out in Seapink Lane.
Across the Garden of Remembrance? No,
That would be blasphemy and bring bad luck.
Well then, I'm *for* it. Andrew's at me first,
He pinions me in that especial grip
His brother learned in Kobë from a Jap
(No chance for me against the Japanese).
Willie arrives and winds me with a punch
Plum in the tummy, grips the other arm.
'You're to be booted. Hold him steady, chaps!'
A wait for taking aim. Oh trees and sky!
Then crack against the column of my spine,
Blackness and breathlessness and sick with pain
I stumble on the asphalt. Off they go
Away, away, thank God, and out of sight
So that I lie quite still and climb to sense
Too out of breath and strength to make a sound.

Now over Polegate vastly sets the sun;
Dark rise the Downs from darker looking elms,
And out of Southern railway trains to tea
Run happy boys down various Station Roads,
Satchels of homework jogging on their backs,
So trivial and so healthy in the shade
Of these enormous Downs. And when they're home,
When the Post-Toasties mixed with Golden Shred
Make for the kiddies such a scrumptious feast,
Does Mum, the Persil-user, still believe
That there's no Devil and that youth is bliss?
As certain as the sun behind the Downs
And quite as plain to see, the Devil walks.

Death in Leamington, by John Betjeman, 1906 – 84

She died in the upstairs bedroom
By the light of the ev'ning star
That shone through the plate glass window
From over Leamington Spa.

Beside her the lonely crochet
Lay patiently and unstirred,
But the fingers that would have work'd it
Were dead as the spoken word.

And Nurse came in with the tea-things
Breast high 'mid the stands and chairs-
But Nurse was alone with her own little soul,
And the things were alone with theirs.

She bolted the big round window,
She let the blinds unroll,
She set a match to the mantle,
She covered the fire with coal.

And "Tea!" she said in a tiny voice
"Wake up! It's nearly *five*."
Oh! Chintzy, chintzy cheeriness,
Half dead and half alive.

Do you know that the stucco is peeling?
Do you know that the heart will stop?
From those yellow Italianate arches
Do you hear the plaster drop?

Nurse looked at the silent bedstead,
At the gray, decaying face,
As the calm of a Leamington ev'ning
Drifted into the place.

She moved the table of bottles
Away from the bed to the wall;
And tiptoeing gently over the stairs
Turned down the gas in the hall.

Section VIII

15 Hymns

Fifteen Hymns

Page

1. The Russian Contakion of the Departed, which
   probably originated in the Byzantine Empire in
   the sixth century A.D.   132

2. God be in my Head, from the Sarum Psalter,
   translated by the Revd G.H.Palmer, 1846 – 1926   132

3. Teach me, my God and King by George Herbert,
                                    1593–1633   133

4. Who would true valour see by John Bunyan,
                                    1628 – 1688   134

5. A metrical version of Psalm 23, as in the Scottish
   Metrical Psalms authorized by the Church of Scotland
   in 1650   135

6. Jerusalem by William Blake, 1757 – 1827   136

7. Dear Lord and Father of Mankind by John Whittier,
                                    1807–93   137

8. There is a green hill far away by Mrs C. F. Alexander,
                                    1818 – 95   138

9. Say not the struggle nought availeth by A. H. Clough,
                                    1819 – 61   139

10. Immortal, Invisible, by W. Chalmers Smith,
                                    1824 – 1908   140

11. In the bleak midwinter by Christina Rossetti,
                                    1830 – 1894   141

12. I vow to thee, my country by Sir Cecil Spring Rice,
                                    1859 – 1918   143

13. In no strange land by Francis Thompson, 1859 – 1907   144

14. Lord of the Dance by Sydney Carter, 1915 – 2004   145

15. Friday Morning by Sydney Carter, 1915 – 2004   146

The Russian Contakion of the Departed,
which probably originated in the Eastern Roman Empire, also known as the Byzantine Empire, in the sixth century A.D.

Give rest, O Christ, to thy servant with thy saints,
Where sorrow and pain are no more,
Neither sighing but life everlasting.

Thou only art immortal, the creator and maker of man,
And we are mortal formed from the dust of the earth,

And unto earth shall we return,
For so thou didst ordain when thou created'st me,
Saying: 'Dust thou art und unto dust shalt thou return.'

All we go down to the dust,
And weeping o'er the grave we make our song:
'Alleluia, Alleluia, Alleluia.'

Give rest, O Christ, to thy servant with thy saints,
Where sorrow and pain are no more,
Neither sighing but life everlasting.

God be in my Head, from the Sarum Psalter, 1538.

God be in my head, and in my understanding;
God be in mine eyes, and in my looking;
God be in my mouth, and in my speaking;
God be in my heart, and in my thinking;
God be at mine end, and at my departing.

Teach me, my God and King,
by George Herbert, 1593 – 1627.

Teach me, my God and King,
in all things thee to see,
and what I do in anything
to do it as for thee.

A man that looks on glass,
on it may stay his eye;
or if he pleaseth, through it pass,
and then the heaven espy.

All may of thee partake;
nothing can be so mean,
which with this tincture, "for thy sake",
will not grow bright and clean.

A servant with this clause
makes drudgery divine:
who sweeps a room, as for thy laws,
makes that and the action fine.

This is the famous stone
that turneth all to gold;
for that which God doth touch and own
cannot for less be told.

A metrical version of Psalm 23

In Scotland, where for many years the only hymns permitted in Presbyterian services were metrical versions of the psalms, the version below, from the collection of Scottish Metrical Psalms authorized by the Church of Scotland in 1650, was based on a translation by a certain Thomas Sternhold nearly a hundred years earlier, in 1565.

The sixteenth century English translation of Psalm 23 by Miles Coverdale, used in the Book of Common Prayer, is on page 24.

> The Lord's my shepherd, I'll not want.
>   He makes me down to lie
> In pastures green: he leadeth me
>   the quiet waters by.
>
> My soul he doth restore again;
>   and me to walk doth make
> Within the paths of righteousness,
>   ev'n for his own name's sake.
>
> Yea, though I walk in death's dark vale,
>   yet will I fear none ill:
> For thou art with me; and thy rod
>   and staff me comfort still.
>
> My table thou hast furnishèd
>   in presence of my foes;
> My head thou dost with oil anoint,
>   and my cup overflows.
>
> Goodness and mercy all my life
>   shall surely follow me:
> And in God's house for evermore
>   my dwelling-place shall be.

To be a Pilgim, by John Bunyan, 1628 – 88
(The original version, as in 'Pilgrim's Progress')

Who would true valour see,
Let him come hither;
One here will constant be,
Come wind, come weather;
There's no discouragement
Shall make him once relent
His first avowed intent
To be a pilgrim.

Whoso beset him round
With dismal stories,
Do but themselves confound;
His strength the more is.
No lion can him fright,
He'll with a giant fight,
But he will have the right
To be a pilgrim.

Hobgoblin nor foul fiend
Can daunt his spirit;
He knows he at the end
Shall life inherit.
Then fancies fly away,
He'll not fear what men say;
He'll labour night and day
To be a pilgrim.

Jerusalem, by William Blake, 1757 – 1827

And did those feet in ancient time
Walk upon England's mountains green?
And was the holy Lamb of God
On England's pleasant pastures seen?
And did the countenance divine
Shine forth upon our clouded hills?
And was Jerusalem builded here
Among those dark satanic mills?

Bring me my bow of burning gold!
Bring me my arrows of desire!
Bring me my spear! O clouds unfold!
Bring me my chariot of fire!
I will not cease from mental fight,
Nor shall my sword sleep in my hand,
Till we have built Jerusalem
In England's green and pleasant land.

Dear Lord and Father of Mankind,
by John G. Whittier, 1807 – 92

Dear Lord and Father of mankind,
forgive our foolish ways;
reclothe us in our rightful mind,
in purer lives thy service find,
in deeper reverence, praise.

In simple trust like theirs who heard
beside the Syrian sea
the gracious calling of the Lord,
let us, like them, without a word
rise up and follow thee.

O Sabbath rest by Galilee,
O calm of hills above,
where Jesus knelt to share with thee
the silence of eternity,
interpreted by love!

Drop thy still dews of quietness,
till all our strivings cease;
take from our souls the strain and stress,
and let our ordered lives confess
the beauty of thy peace.

Breathe through the heats of our desire
thy coolness and thy balm;
let sense be dumb, let flesh retire;
speak through the earthquake, wind, and fire,
O still, small voice of calm!

There is a green hill far away,
by Mrs C.F.Alexander, 1818 – 95

Mrs Alexander, born Cecil Frances Humphreys, was married for forty-five years to the Bishop of Derry, later Archbishop of Armagh. She wrote a large number of hymns, among them Once in Royal David's City *and* All Things Bright and Beautiful. *This one was inspired by the green hills outside the walls of Derry.*

There is a green hill far away,
without a city wall,
where the dear Lord was crucified,
who died to save us all.

We may not know, we cannot tell,
what pains he had to bear,
but we believe it was for us
he hung and suffered there.

He died that we might be forgiven,
he died to make us good,
that we might go at last to heaven,
saved by his precious blood.

There was no other good enough
to pay the price of sin;
he only could unlock the gate
of heaven, and let us in.

O dearly, dearly has he loved,
and we must love him too,
and trust in his redeeming blood,
and try his works to do.

Say not the struggle nought availeth,
by A.H.Clough, 1819 – 61

Hope, which is the subject of this hymn, is probably the most neglected of St Paul's three great theological virtues: Faith, Hope and Love.

In the Second World War, from the fall of France in June of 1940 until Hitler attacked Russia exactly a year later, Great Britain stood alone in Europe. The USA was not yet involved, but towards the end of 1941 Winston Churchill, looking for help from the USA, spoke on the radio to the British people, quoting the last verse of this hymn. It was immensely moving.

> Say not the struggle naught availeth,
>   The labour and the wounds are vain,
> The enemy faints not, nor faileth,
>   And as things have been they remain.
>
> If hopes were dupes, fears may be liars;
>   It may be, in yon smoke conceal'd,
> Your comrades chase e'en now the fliers,
>   And, but for you, possess the field.
>
> For while the tired waves, vainly breaking,
>   Seem here no painful inch to gain,
> Far back, through creeks and inlets making,
>   Comes silent, flooding in, the main.
>
> And not by eastern windows only,
>   When daylight comes, comes in the light;
> In front the sun climbs slow, how slowly!
>   But westward, look, the land is bright!

Immortal, Invisible, God Only Wise,
by W. Chalmers Smith, 1824 – 1908

The Revd Dr Walter Chalmers Smith was a minister of the Free Church of Scotland who also wrote a number of hymns and poems. Immortal, Invisible, God Only Wise *is the most famous of his hymns. In it he attempts to express the inexpressible and does that probably more successfully than anyone else writing in the tradition of the Western Catholic and Protestant churches.*

Towards the end of his life he was the Moderator of the Free Church of Scotland.

> Immortal, invisible, God only wise,
> In light inaccessible hid from our eyes,
> Most blessèd, most glorious, the Ancient of Days,
> Almighty, victorious, thy great name we praise.
>
> Unresting, unhasting, and silent as light,
> Nor wanting, nor wasting, thou rulest in might;
> Thy justice like mountains high soaring above
> Thy clouds which are fountains of goodness and love.
>
> To all life thou givest - to both great and small;
> In all life thou livest, the true life of all;
> We blossom and flourish as leaves on the tree,
> And wither and perish - but naught changeth thee.
>
> Great Father of Glory, pure Father of Light;
> Thine Angels adore thee, all veiling their sight;
> All laud we would render: O help us to see
> 'Tis only the splendour of light hideth thee.

In the bleak midwinter, by Christina Rossetti, 1830 – 94

Of all the innumerable Christmas Carols which are worth learning and remembering I have chosen this one.

It was first published in 1872, and was set to music in the early twentieth century by both Gustav Holst and Harold Edwin Darke. Both settings are beautiful, and it is difficult to choose between them.

> In the bleak mid-winter
>   Frosty wind made moan,
> Earth stood hard as iron,
>   Water like a stone;
> Snow had fallen, snow on snow,
>   Snow on snow,
> In the bleak mid-winter
>   Long ago.
>
> Our God, Heaven cannot hold Him
>   Nor earth sustain;
> Heaven and earth shall flee away
>   When He comes to reign:
> In the bleak mid-winter
>   A stable-place sufficed
> The Lord God Almighty,
>   Jesus Christ.
>
> Enough for Him, whom cherubim
>   Worship night and day,
> A breastful of milk
>   And a mangerful of hay;
> Enough for Him, whom angels
>   Fall down before,
> The ox and ass and camel
>   Which adore.

Angels and archangels
   May have gathered there,
Cherubim and seraphim
   Thronged the air –
But only His mother
   In her maiden bliss,
Worshipped the Beloved
   With a kiss.

What can I give Him,
   Poor as I am?
If I were a shepherd
   I would bring a lamb,
If I were a wise man
   I would do my part,
Yet what I can I give Him,
   Give my heart.

I vow to thee my country,
by Sir Cecil Spring Rice, 1859 - 1918

I vow to thee my country
All earthly things above,
Entire and whole and perfect
The service of my love,
The love that asks no question,
The love that stands the test,
That lays upon the altar
The dearest and the best,
The love that never falters,
The love that pays the price,
The love that makes undaunted
The final sacrifice.

And there's another country
I've heard of long ago,
Most dear to them that love her,
Most great to them that know.
We may not count her armies.
We may not see her king.
Her fortress is a faithful heart,
Her pride is suffering,
And soul by soul and silently
Her shining bounds increase,
And her ways are ways of gentleness
And all her paths are peace.

In no strange land, by Francis Thompson, 1859 – 1907

When I first encountered this hymn in the Christ's Hospital chapel at the age of ten, it puzzled me. By the time I left school eight years later it had influenced my thinking more than any other single hymn.

O world invisible, we view thee,
O world intangible, we touch thee,
O world unknowable, we know thee,
Inapprehensible, we clutch thee!

Does the fish soar to find the ocean,
The eagle plunge to find the air—
That we ask of the stars in motion
If they have rumour of thee there?

Not where the wheeling systems darken,
And our benumbed conceiving soars!—
The drift of pinions, would we hearken,
Beats at our own clay-shuttered doors.

The angels keep their ancient places;—
Turn but a stone and start a wing!
'Tis ye, 'tis your estrangèd faces,
That miss the many-splendoured thing.

But (when so sad thou canst not sadder)
Cry;—and upon thy so sore loss
Shall shine the traffic of Jacob's ladder
Pitched betwixt Heaven and Charing Cross.

Yea, in the night, my Soul, my daughter,
Cry,—clinging to Heaven by the hems;
And lo, Christ walking on the water,
Not of Genesareth, but Thames!

Lord of the Dance, by Sydney Carter, 1915 – 2004

Sydney Carter was born in Camden Town and educated at Christ's Hospital and at Balliol College, Oxford, where he read History. In the Second World War he served in the Friends' Ambulance Unit in the Mediterranean. After the war he had a successful career writing lyrics for the popular entertainer, Donald Swann, who had served with him in the Friends' Ambulance Unit in the war, and he also wrote a number of immensely popular, though sometimes controversial, hymns. Shortly after he was eighty a survey found that two of his hymns were among the ten most popular for singing in school assemblies. One More Step *was placed first and* Lord of the Dance *fifth.*

A few years later he began to suffer from Alzheimer's disease. Stainer & Bell's 'Sydney Carter's Lord of the Dance and other songs and poems' *describes how his friend, Rabbi Lionel Blue, wrote that* 'Our contact was a thin thread of memory of his songs. I would start singing them, and he would joyfully join in, and for a short while we were one again. We squeezed hands and I would leave him as he continued singing.'

I danced in the morning when the world was begun,
   And I danced in the moon and the stars and the sun,
And I came down from heaven and I danced on the earth,
   At Bethlehem I had my birth.
Refrain: *Dance, then, wherever you may be;*
       I am the Lord of the Dance, said he,
       And I'll lead you all, wherever you may be,
       And I'll lead you all in the Dance, said he.

I danced for the scribe and the Pharisee,
   But they would not dance and they wouldn't follow me.
I danced for the fishermen, for James and John -
   They came with me and the dance went on.
Refrain...

I danced on the Sabbath and I cured the lame;
  The holy people said it was a shame.
They whipped and they stripped and they hung me on high,
  They left me there on a Cross to die.
Refrain:

I danced on a Friday when the sky turned black –
  It's hard to dance with the devil on your back.
They buried my body and they thought I'd gone,
  But I am the Dance, and I still go on.
Refrain...

They cut me down and I leapt up high;
  I am the life that'll never, never die;
I'll live in you if you'll live in me -
  I am the Lord of the Dance, said he.
Refrain...

Friday Morning, by Sydney Carter, 1915 – 2004

While Lord of the Dance *is very popular and much sung in church and school assemblies,* Friday Morning *is far less well known. At the time of its publication it caused widespread controversy both in Britain and America on account of its ironic refrain:* 'It's God they ought to crucify instead of you and me'.

It was on a Friday morning that they took me from the cell
and I saw they had a carpenter to crucify as well.
You can blame it on to Pilate,
You can blame it on the Jews,
You can blame it on the Devil.
It's God I accuse.
It's God they ought to crucify instead of you and me,
I said to the carpenter, a-hanging on the tree.

You can blame it on to Adam,
You can blame it on to Eve,
You can blame it on the apple,
but that I can't believe.
It was God that made the Devil
And the woman and the man,
And there wouldn't be an apple
If it wasn't in the plan.
It's God they ought to crucify instead of you and me,
I said to the carpenter, a-hanging on the tree.

Now Barabbas was a killer
And they let Barabbas go,
But you are being crucified
For nothing that I know,
And your God is up in Heaven
And He doesn't do a thing,
With a million angels watching,
And they never move a wing.
It's God they ought to crucify instead of you and me,
I said to the carpenter, a-hanging on the tree.

To hell with Jehovah,
To the carpenter I said
I wish that a carpenter
had made the world instead.
Goodbye and good luck to you.
Our ways will soon divide.
Remember me tomorrow,
The man you hung beside.
It's God they ought to crucify instead of you and me,
I said to the carpenter, a-hanging on the tree.

Section IX

15 Longer Pieces

Fifteen Longer Pieces

Page

1. The Prologue to *The Life of Henry the Fifth*
   by William Shakespeare, 1564 – 1616   150

2. Henry V at the siege of Harfleur, *Act 3, scene 1*   152

3. Henry V before the battle of Agincourt,
   Act 4, scene 3   153

4. From a speech by Jacques in *As You Like It, Act II,
   scene VII,* also by William Shakespeare   155

5. To a Mouse, on Turning Her Up in Her Nest With the
   Plough, November, 1785, by Robert Burns,
   1759 – 1796   156

6. Kubla Khan by Samuel Taylor Coleridge,
   1772 – 1834   158

7. Ode on a Grecian Urn by John Keats, 1795 – 1821   160

8. Ode to a Nightingale by John Keats, 1795 – 1821   162

9. My Last Duchess by Robert Browning, 1812 – 1889   165

10. If by Rudyard Kipling, 1865 – 1936   167

11. The Roman Centurion's Song, also by
    Rudyard Kipling   168

12. The South Country by Hilaire Belloc, 1870 – 1953   170

13. The Love Song of J. Alfred Prufrock by T. S. Eliot,
    1888 – 1965   172

14. Thomas Becket's soliloquy at the end of Act I
    of *Murder in the Cathedral* by T.S.Eliot,
    1888 – 1965   177

15. Father and Son: 1939 by William Plomer,
    1903 – 1973   179

The Prologue to Henry V,
by William Shakespeare, 1564 – 1616

In the autumn of 1945, when I was still eleven years old, with the Second World War recently over and near the beginning of my second year at Christ's Hospital, the whole school, 830 boys, marched the three miles into Horsham to go to the Odeon cinema to see the film of Henry the Fifth, *which had been released the previous year. It was directed by Lawrence Olivier, who also starred in the title role.*

It seemed to me as if Shakespeare had foreseen the Second World War and written a play with echoes of what was to come. When it was over we marched back, and that evening, when I went to bed, I started learning it. That is, with a torch under my blankets, I started to learn the Prologue, *and later went on to learn Henry's speech before the walls of Harfleur and his speech the evening before the battle of Agincourt.*

O for a Muse of fire, that would ascend
The brightest heaven of invention,
A kingdom for a stage, princes to act
And monarchs to behold the swelling scene!
Then should the warlike Harry, like himself,
Assume the port of Mars; and at his heels,
Leash'd in like hounds, should famine, sword and fire
Crouch for employment. But pardon, gentles all,
The flat unraised spirits that have dared
On this unworthy scaffold to bring forth
So great an object: can this cockpit hold
The vasty fields of France? or may we cram
Within this wooden O the very casques
That did affright the air at Agincourt?
O, pardon! since a crooked figure may
Attest in little place a million;
And let us, ciphers to this great accompt,
On your imaginary forces work.

Suppose within the girdle of these walls
Are now confined two mighty monarchies,
Whose high upreared and abutting fronts
The perilous narrow ocean parts asunder:
Piece out our imperfections with your thoughts;
Into a thousand parts divide one man,
And make imaginary puissance;
Think when we talk of horses, that you see them
Printing their proud hoofs i' the receiving earth;
For 'tis your thoughts that now must deck our kings,
Carry them here and there, jumping o'er times,
Turning the accomplishment of many years
Into an hour-glass: for the which supply,
Admit me Chorus to this history;
Who, Prologue-like, your humble patience pray,
Gently to hear, kindly to judge, our play.

Henry V addressing his troops at the siege of Harfleur, from Shakespeare's *The Life of Henry the Fifth,* Act 3, scene 1.

Once more unto the breach, dear friends, once more;
Or close the wall up with our English dead.
In peace there's nothing so becomes a man
As modest stillness and humility:
But when the blast of war blows in our ears,
Then imitate the action of the tiger;
Stiffen the sinews, summon up the blood,
Disguise fair nature with hard-favour'd rage;
Then lend the eye a terrible aspect;
Let it pry through the portage of the head
Like the brass cannon; let the brow o'erwhelm it
As fearfully as doth a galled rock
O'erhang and jutty his confounded base,
Swill'd with the wild and wasteful ocean.
Now set the teeth and stretch the nostril wide,
Hold hard the breath and bend up every spirit
To his full height. On, on, you noblest English,
Whose blood is fet from fathers of war-proof!
Fathers that, like so many Alexanders,
Have in these parts from morn till even fought
And sheathed their swords for lack of argument:
Dishonour not your mothers; now attest
That those whom you call'd fathers did beget you.
Be copy now to men of grosser blood,
And teach them how to war. And you, good yeomen,
Whose limbs were made in England, show us here
The mettle of your pasture; let us swear
That you are worth your breeding, which I doubt not;
For there is none of you so mean and base,
That hath not noble lustre in your eyes.
I see you stand like greyhounds in the slips,
Straining upon the start. The game's afoot:
Follow your spirit, and upon this charge
Cry 'God for Harry, England, and Saint George!'

Henry V, speaking before the battle of Agincourt of 1415, in Act 4, scene 3, of Shakespeare's *The Life of Henry the Fifth*, replying to the wish of the Duke of Westmorland that they had another ten thousand men with which to face the French army.

WESTMORLAND. O that we now had here
But one ten thousand of those men in England
That do no work to-day!

KING. What's he that wishes so?
My cousin, Westmorland? No, my fair cousin;
If we are mark'd to die, we are enough
To do our country loss; and if to live,
The fewer men, the greater share of honour.
God's will! I pray thee, wish not one man more.
By Jove, I am not covetous for gold,
Nor care I who doth feed upon my cost;
It yearns me not if men my garments wear;
Such outward things dwell not in my desires.
But if it be a sin to covet honour,
I am the most offending soul alive.
No, faith, my coz, wish not a man from England.
God's peace! I would not lose so great an honour
As one man more methinks would share from me
For the best hope I have. O, do not wish one more!
Rather proclaim it, Westmorland, through my host,
That he which hath no stomach to this fight,
Let him depart; his passport shall be made,
And crowns for convoy put into his purse;
We would not die in that man's company
That fears his fellowship to die with us.

This day is call'd the feast of Crispian.
He that outlives this day, and comes safe home,
Will stand a tip-toe when this day is nam'd,
And rouse him at the name of Crispian.
He that shall live this day, and see old age,
Will yearly on the vigil feast his neighbours,
And say "To-morrow is Saint Crispian."
Then will he strip his sleeve and show his scars,
And say "These wounds I had on Crispin's day."

Old men forget; yet all shall be forgot,
But he'll remember, with advantages,
What feats he did that day. Then shall our names,
Familiar in his mouth as household words—
Harry the King, Bedford and Exeter,
Warwick and Talbot, Salisbury and Gloucester—
Be in their flowing cups freshly rememb'red.
This story shall the good man teach his son;
And Crispin Crispian shall ne'er go by,
From this day to the ending of the world,
But we in it shall be rememberèd—
We few, we happy few, we band of brothers;
For he to-day that sheds his blood with me
Shall be my brother; be he ne'er so vile,
This day shall gentle his condition;
And gentlemen in England now a-bed
Shall think themselves accurs'd they were not here,
And hold their manhoods cheap whiles any speaks
That fought with us upon Saint Crispin's day.

All the world's a stage, an extract from a speech by one of the courtiers, Jaques, in Act II, scene VII of *As You Like It*, by William Shakespeare

All the world's a stage,
And all the men and women merely players;
They have their exits and their entrances;
And one man in his time plays many parts,
His acts being seven ages. At first the infant,
Mewling and puking in the nurse's arms;
And then the whining school-boy, with his satchel
And shining morning face, creeping like snail
Unwillingly to school. And then the lover,
Sighing like furnace, with a woeful ballad
Made to his mistress' eyebrow. Then a soldier,
Full of strange oaths, and bearded like the pard,
Jealous in honour, sudden and quick in quarrel,
Seeking the bubble reputation
Even in the cannon's mouth. And then the justice,
In fair round belly with good capon lin'd,
With eyes severe and beard of formal cut,
Full of wise saws and modern instances;
And so he plays his part. The sixth age shifts
Into the lean and slipper'd pantaloon,
With spectacles on nose and pouch on side;
His youthful hose, well sav'd, a world too wide
For his shrunk shank; and his big manly voice,
Turning again toward childish treble, pipes
And whistles in his sound. Last scene of all,
That ends this strange eventful history,
Is second childishness and mere oblivion;
Sans teeth, sans eyes, sans taste, sans everything.

To a Mouse, on Turning Her Up in Her Nest With the Plough, November, 1785, by Robert Burns, 1759 – 1796

Wee, sleekit, cow'rin', tim'rous beastie,
O, what a panic's in thy breastie!
Thou need na start awa sae hasty,
Wi' bickering brattle!
I wad be laith to rin an' chase thee
Wi' murd'ring pattle!

I'm truly sorry man's dominion
Has broken nature's social union,
An' justifies that ill opinion,
What makes thee startle
At me, thy poor, earth-born companion,
An' fellow-mortal!

I doubt na, whiles, but thou may thieve;
What then? poor beastie, thou maun live!
A daimen icker in a thrave
'S a sma' request;
I'll get a blessin wi' the lave,
An' never miss't!

Thy wee bit housie, too, in ruin!
It's silly wa's the win's are strewin!
An' naething, now, to big a new ane,
O' foggage green!
An' bleak December's winds ensuin,
Baith snell an' keen!

Thou saw the fields laid bare an' waste,
An' weary winter comin' fast,
An' cozie here, beneath the blast,
Thou thought to dwell -
Till crash! the cruel coulter past
Out thro' thy cell.

That wee bit heap o' leaves an' stibble,
Has cost thee mony a weary nibble!
Now thou's turn'd out, for a' thy trouble,
But house or hald,
To thole the winter's sleety dribble,
An' cranreuch cauld!

But Mousie, thou art no thy lane,
In proving foresight may be vain;
The best-laid schemes o' mice an' men
Gang aft agley,
An' lea'e us nought but grief an' pain,
For promis'd joy!

Still thou art blest, compar'd wi' me;
The present only toucheth thee:
But och! I backward cast my e'e,
On prospects drear!
An' forward, tho' I canna see,
I guess an' fear!

Kubla Khan,
by Samuel Taylor Coleridge, 1772 – 1834

In Xanadu did Kubla Khan
A stately pleasure-dome decree:
Where Alph, the sacred river, ran
Through caverns measureless to man
Down to a sunless sea.

So twice five miles of fertile ground
With walls and towers were girdled round;
And there were gardens bright with sinuous rills,
Where blossomed many an incense-bearing tree;
And here were forests ancient as the hills,
Enfolding sunny spots of greenery.

But oh! that deep romantic chasm which slanted
Down the green hill athwart a cedarn cover!
A savage place! as holy and enchanted
As e'er beneath a waning moon was haunted
By woman wailing for her demon-lover!

And from this chasm, with ceaseless turmoil seething,
As if this earth in fast thick pants were breathing,
A mighty fountain momently was forced:
Amid whose swift half-intermitted burst
Huge fragments vaulted like rebounding hail,
Or chaffy grain beneath the thresher's flail:

And mid these dancing rocks at once and ever
It flung up momently the sacred river.
Five miles meandering with a mazy motion
Through wood and dale the sacred river ran,
Then reached the caverns measureless to man,
And sank in tumult to a lifeless ocean;

And 'mid this tumult Kubla heard from far
Ancestral voices prophesying war!

  The shadow of the dome of pleasure
  Floated midway on the waves;
  Where was heard the mingled measure
  From the fountain and the caves.
It was a miracle of rare device,
A sunny pleasure-dome with caves of ice!

  A damsel with a dulcimer
  In a vision once I saw:
  It was an Abyssinian maid
  And on her dulcimer she played,
  Singing of Mount Abora.

  Could I revive within me
  Her symphony and song,
  To such a deep delight 'twould win me,
That with music loud and long,
I would build that dome in air,
That sunny dome! those caves of ice!

And all who heard should see them there,
And all should cry, Beware! Beware!
His flashing eyes, his floating hair!
Weave a circle round him thrice,
And close your eyes with holy dread
For he on honey-dew hath fed,
And drunk the milk of Paradise.

Ode on a Grecian Urn, by John Keats, 1795 – 1821

Thou still unravish'd bride of quietness,
   Thou foster-child of silence and slow time,
Sylvan historian, who canst thus express
   A flowery tale more sweetly than our rhyme:
What leaf-fring'd legend haunts about thy shape
   Of deities or mortals, or of both,
      In Tempe or the dales of Arcady?
   What men or gods are these? What maidens loth?
What mad pursuit? What struggle to escape?
      What pipes and timbrels? What wild ecstasy?

Heard melodies are sweet, but those unheard
   Are sweeter; therefore, ye soft pipes, play on;
Not to the sensual ear, but, more endear'd,
   Pipe to the spirit ditties of no tone:
Fair youth, beneath the trees, thou canst not leave
   Thy song, nor ever can those trees be bare;
      Bold Lover, never, never canst thou kiss,
Though winning near the goal – yet do not grieve;
   She cannot fade, though thou hast not thy bliss,
      For ever wilt thou love, and she be fair!

Ah, happy, happy boughs! that cannot shed
   Your leaves, nor ever bid the Spring adieu;
And, happy melodist, unwearied,
   For ever piping songs for ever new;
More happy love! more happy, happy love!
   For ever warm and still to be enjoy'd,
      For ever panting, and for ever young;
All breathing human passion far above,
   That leaves a heart high-sorrowful and cloy'd,
      A burning forehead, and a parching tongue.

Who are these coming to the sacrifice?
  To what green altar, O mysterious priest,
Lead'st thou that heifer lowing at the skies,
  And all her silken flanks with garlands drest?
What little town by river or sea shore,
  Or mountain-built with peaceful citadel,
    Is emptied of its folk, this pious morn?
And, little town, thy streets for evermore
  Will silent be; and not a soul to tell
    Why thou art desolate, can e'er return.

O Attic shape! Fair attitude! with brede
  Of marble men and maidens overwrought,
With forest branches and the trodden weed;
  Thou, silent form, dost tease us out of thought
As doth eternity. Cold Pastoral!
  When old age shall this generation waste,
    Thou shalt remain, in midst of other woe
Than ours, a friend to man, to whom thou say'st,
  "Beauty is truth, truth beauty,—that is all
    Ye know on earth, and all ye need to know."

Ode to a Nightingale, by John Keats, 1795 – 1821

My heart aches, and a drowsy numbness pains
  My sense, as though of hemlock I had drunk,
Or emptied some dull opiate to the drains
  One minute past, and Lethe-wards had sunk:
'Tis not through envy of thy happy lot,
  But being too happy in thine happiness,—
    That thou, light-winged Dryad of the trees,
      In some melodious plot
  Of beechen green, and shadows numberless,
    Singest of summer in full-throated ease.

O, for a draught of vintage! that hath been
  Cool'd a long age in the deep-delved earth,
Tasting of Flora and the country green,
  Dance, and Provençal song, and sunburnt mirth!
O for a beaker full of the warm South,
  Full of the true, the blushful Hippocrene,
    With beaded bubbles winking at the brim,
      And purple-stained mouth;
  That I might drink, and leave the world unseen,
    And with thee fade away into the forest dim:

Fade far away, dissolve, and quite forget
  What thou among the leaves hast never known,
The weariness, the fever, and the fret
  Here, where men sit and hear each other groan;
Where palsy shakes a few, sad, last grey hairs,
  Where youth grows pale, and spectre-thin, and dies;
    Where but to think is to be full of sorrow
      And leaden-eyed despairs,
  Where Beauty cannot keep her lustrous eyes,
    Or new Love pine at them beyond to-morrow.

Away! away! for I will fly to thee,
  Not charioted by Bacchus and his pards,
But on the viewless wings of Poesy,
  Though the dull brain perplexes and retards:
Already with thee! tender is the night,
  And haply the Queen-Moon is on her throne,
    Cluster'd around by all her starry Fays;
      But here there is no light,
  Save what from heaven is with the breezes blown
    Through verdurous glooms and winding mossy ways.

I cannot see what flowers are at my feet,
  Nor what soft incense hangs upon the boughs,
But, in embalmed darkness, guess each sweet
  Wherewith the seasonable month endows
The grass, the thicket, and the fruit-tree wild;
  White hawthorn, and the pastoral eglantine;
    Fast fading violets cover'd up in leaves;
      And mid-May's eldest child,
  The coming musk-rose, full of dewy wine,
    The murmurous haunt of flies on summer eves.

Darkling I listen; and, for many a time
  I have been half in love with easeful Death,
Call'd him soft names in many a mused rhyme,
  To take into the air my quiet breath;
    Now more than ever seems it rich to die,
To cease upon the midnight with no pain,
    While thou art pouring forth thy soul abroad
      In such an ecstasy!
  Still wouldst thou sing, and I have ears in vain—
    To thy high requiem become a sod.

Thou wast not born for death, immortal Bird!
No hungry generations tread thee down;
The voice I hear this passing night was heard
In ancient days by emperor and clown:
Perhaps the self-same song that found a path
Through the sad heart of Ruth, when, sick for home,
She stood in tears amid the alien corn;
The same that oft-times hath
Charm'd magic casements, opening on the foam
Of perilous seas, in faery lands forlorn.

Forlorn! the very word is like a bell
To toll me back from thee to my sole self!
Adieu! the fancy cannot cheat so well
As she is fam'd to do, deceiving elf.
Adieu! adieu! thy plaintive anthem fades
Past the near meadows, over the still stream,
Up the hill-side; and now 'tis buried deep
In the next valley-glades:
Was it a vision, or a waking dream?
Fled is that music:—Do I wake or sleep?

My Last Duchess, by Robert Browning, 1812 – 1889

That's my last Duchess painted on the wall,
Looking as if she were alive. I call
That piece a wonder, now: Frà Pandolf's hands
Worked busily a day, and there she stands.
Will't please you sit and look at her? I said
"Frà Pandolf" by design, for never read
Strangers like you that pictured countenance,
The depth and passion of its earnest glance,
But to myself they turned (since none puts by
The curtain I have drawn for you, but I)
And seemed as they would ask me, if they durst,
How such a glance came there; so, not the first
Are you to turn and ask thus. Sir, 'twas not
Her husband's presence only, called that spot
Of joy into the Duchess' cheek: perhaps
Frà Pandolf chanced to say "Her mantle laps
Over my lady's wrist too much," or "Paint
Must never hope to reproduce the faint
Half-flush that dies along her throat." Such stuff
Was courtesy, she thought, and cause enough
For calling up that spot of joy. She had
A heart–how shall I say?–too soon made glad,
Too easily impressed; she liked whate'er
She looked on, and her looks went everywhere.
Sir, 'twas all one! My favour at her breast,
The dropping of the daylight in the West,
The bough of cherries some officious fool
Broke in the orchard for her, the white mule
She rode with round the terrace - all and each
Would draw from her alike the approving speech,
Or blush, at least. She thanked men, - good! but thanked
Somehow -I know not how - as if she ranked
My gift of a nine-hundred-years-old name
With anybody's gift. Who'd stoop to blame
This sort of trifling? Even had you skill

In speech - (which I have not) - to make your will
Quite clear to such an one, and say, "Just this
Or that in you disgusts me; here you miss,
Or there exceed the mark" - and if she let
Herself be lessoned so, nor plainly set
Her wits to yours, forsooth, and made excuse–
E'en then would be some stooping; and I choose
Never to stoop. Oh sir, she smiled, no doubt,
Whene'er I passed her; but who passed without
Much the same smile? This grew; I gave commands;
Then all smiles stopped together. There she stands
As if alive. Will't please you rise? We'll meet
The company below, then. I repeat,
The Count your master's known munificence
Is ample warrant that no just pretence
Of mine for dowry will be disallowed;
Though his fair daughter's self, as I avowed
At starting, is my object. Nay, we'll go
Together down, sir. Notice Neptune, though,
Taming a sea-horse, thought a rarity,
Which Claus of Innsbruck cast in bronze for me.

If, by Rudyard Kipling, 1865 – 1936

If you can keep your head when all about you
Are losing theirs and blaming it on you;
If you can trust yourself when all men doubt you,
But make allowance for their doubting too:
If you can wait and not be tired by waiting,
Or, being lied about, don't deal in lies,
Or being hated don't give way to hating,
And yet don't look too good, nor talk too wise;

If you can dream – and not make dreams your master;
If you can think – and not make thoughts your aim;
If you can meet with Triumph and Disaster
And treat those two impostors just the same;
If you can bear to hear the truth you've spoken
Twisted by knaves to make a trap for fools,
Or watch the things you gave your life to, broken,
And stoop and build'em up with worn-out tools;

If you can make one heap of all your winnings
And risk it on one turn of pitch-and-toss,
And lose, and start again at your beginnings,
And never breathe a word about your loss;
If you can force your heart and nerve and sinew
To serve your turn long after they are gone,
And so hold on when there is nothing in you
Except the Will which says to them: 'Hold on!'

If you can talk with crowds and keep your virtue,
Or walk with Kings – nor lose the common touch,
If neither foes nor loving friends can hurt you,
If all men count with you, but none too much:
If you can fill the unforgiving minute
With sixty seconds' worth of distance run,
Yours is the Earth and everything that's in it,
And – which is more – you'll be a Man, my son!

The Roman Centurion's Song,
by Rudyard Kipling, 1865 – 1936

It may be worth knowing the modern names for some of the places and other things referred to in this poem:

Portus Itius *was a Roman port, probably near Calais or Boulogne.*
Vectis *is the Latin name for the Isle of Wight.*
The wall *is Hadrian's Wall, built in the early second century A.D. and running from the Solway Firth in the West to Wallsend in the East.*
Rhodanus *is the River Rhone.*
Nemausus *is Nime.*
Arelate *is Arles.*
Euroclydon *is the north-east wind.*
The Aurelian Road, *also built in the second century, ran westwards from Rome to the Tyrrhenian Sea, which is the part of the Mediterranean to the west of Italy, and which is here referred to as the Tyrrhene Ocean.*

Legate, I had the news last night - my cohort ordered home
By ships to Portus Itius and thence by road to Rome.
I've marched the companies aboard, the arms are stowed below:
Now let another take my sword. Command me not to go!

I've served in Britain forty years, from Vectis to the Wall,
I have none other home than this, nor any life at all.
Last night I did not understand, but, now the hour draws near
That calls me to my native land, I feel that land is here.

Here where men say my name was made, here where my work
   was done;
Here where my dearest dead are laid - my wife - my wife and
   son;
Here where time, custom, grief and toil, age, memory, service,
   love,
Have rooted me in British soil. Ah, how can I remove?

For me this land, that sea, these airs, those folk and fields suffice.
What purple Southern pomp can match our changeful Northern
   skies,
Black with December snows unshed or pearled with August haze -
The clanging arch of steel-grey March, or June's long-lighted
   days?

You'll follow widening Rhodanus till vine and olive lean
Aslant before the sunny breeze that sweeps Nemausus clean
To Arelate's triple gate; but let me linger on,
Here where our stiff-necked British oaks confront Euroclydon!

You'll take the old Aurelian Road through shore-descending
   pines
Where, blue as any peacock's neck, the Tyrrhene Ocean shines.
You'll go where laurel crowns are won, but - will you e'er forget
The scent of hawthorn in the sun, or bracken in the wet?

Let me work here for Britain's sake - at any task you will -
A marsh to drain, a road to make or native troops to drill.
Some Western camp (I know the Pict) or granite Border keep,
Mid seas of heather derelict, where our old messmates sleep.

Legate, I come to you in tears - My cohort ordered home!
I've served in Britain forty years. What should I do in Rome?
Here is my heart, my soul, my mind - the only life I know.
I cannot leave it all behind. Command me not to go!

The South Country, by Hilaire Belloc, 1870 – 1953

When I am living in the Midlands
That are sodden and unkind,
I light my lamp in the evening:
My work is left behind;
And the great hills of the South Country
Come back into my mind.

The great hills of the South Country
They stand along the sea;
And it's there walking in the high woods
That I could wish to be,
And the men that were boys when I was a boy
Walking along with me.

The men that live in North England
I saw them for a day:
Their hearts are set upon the waste fells,
Their skies are fast and grey;
From their castle-walls a man may see
The mountains far away.

The men that live in West England
They see the Severn strong,
A-rolling on rough water brown
Light aspen leaves along.
They have the secret of the Rocks,
And the oldest kind of song.

But the men that live in the South Country
Are the kindest and most wise,
They get their laughter from the loud surf,
And the faith in their happy eyes
Comes surely from our Sister the Spring
When over the sea she flies;
The violets suddenly bloom at her feet,
She blesses us with surprise.

I never get between the pines
But I smell the Sussex air;
Nor I never come on a belt of sand
But my home is there.
And along the sky the line of the Downs
So noble and so bare.

A lost thing could I never find,
Nor a broken thing mend:
And I fear I shall be all alone
When I get towards the end.
Who will there be to comfort me
Or who will be my friend?

I will gather and carefully make my friends
Of the men of the Sussex Weald;
They watch the stars from silent folds,
They stiffly plough the field.
By them and the God of the South Country
My poor soul shall be healed.

If I ever become a rich man,
Or if ever I grow to be old,
I will build a house with deep thatch
To shelter me from the cold,
And there shall the Sussex songs be sung
And the story of Sussex told.

I will hold my house in the high wood
Within a walk of the sea,
And the men that were boys when I was a boy
Shall sit and drink with me.

The Love Song of J. Alfred Prufrock,
by T.S.Eliot, 1885 – 1965

Let us go then, you and I,
When the evening is spread out against the sky
Like a patient etherized upon a table;
Let us go, through certain half-deserted streets,
The muttering retreats
Of restless nights in one-night cheap hotels
And sawdust restaurants with oyster-shells:
Streets that follow like a tedious argument
Of insidious intent
To lead you to an overwhelming question ...
Oh, do not ask, "What is it?"
Let us go and make our visit.

In the room the women come and go
Talking of Michelangelo.

The yellow fog that rubs its back upon the window-panes,
The yellow smoke that rubs its muzzle on the window-panes,
Licked its tongue into the corners of the evening,
Lingered upon the pools that stand in drains,
Let fall upon its back the soot that falls from chimneys,
Slipped by the terrace, made a sudden leap,
And seeing that it was a soft October night,
Curled once about the house, and fell asleep.

And indeed there will be time
For the yellow smoke that slides along the street,
Rubbing its back upon the window-panes;
There will be time, there will be time
To prepare a face to meet the faces that you meet;
There will be time to murder and create,
And time for all the works and days of hands
That lift and drop a question on your plate;
Time for you and time for me,
And time yet for a hundred indecisions,
And for a hundred visions and revisions,
Before the taking of a toast and tea.

In the room the women come and go
Talking of Michelangelo.

And indeed there will be time
To wonder, "Do I dare?" and, "Do I dare?"
Time to turn back and descend the stair,
With a bald spot in the middle of my hair —
(They will say: "How his hair is growing thin!")
My morning coat, my collar mounting firmly to the chin,
My necktie rich and modest, but asserted by a simple pin —
(They will say: "But how his arms and legs are thin!")
Do I dare
Disturb the universe?
In a minute there is time
For decisions and revisions which a minute will reverse.

For I have known them all already, known them all:
Have known the evenings, mornings, afternoons,
I have measured out my life with coffee spoons;
I know the voices dying with a dying fall
Beneath the music from a farther room.
      So how should I presume?

And I have known the eyes already, known them all—
The eyes that fix you in a formulated phrase,
And when I am formulated, sprawling on a pin,
When I am pinned and wriggling on the wall,
Then how should I begin
To spit out all the butt-ends of my days and ways?
    And how should I presume?

And I have known the arms already, known them all—
Arms that are braceleted and white and bare
(But in the lamplight, downed with light brown hair!)
Is it perfume from a dress
That makes me so digress?
Arms that lie along a table, or wrap about a shawl.
    And should I then presume?
    And how should I begin?

Shall I say, I have gone at dusk through narrow streets
And watched the smoke that rises from the pipes
Of lonely men in shirt-sleeves, leaning out of windows? ...

I should have been a pair of ragged claws
Scuttling across the floors of silent seas.

And the afternoon, the evening, sleeps so peacefully!
Smoothed by long fingers,
Asleep ... tired ... or it malingers,
Stretched on the floor, here beside you and me.
Should I, after tea and cakes and ices,
Have the strength to force the moment to its crisis?
But though I have wept and fasted, wept and prayed,
Though I have seen my head (grown slightly bald) brought in
    upon a platter,
I am no prophet — and here's no great matter;
I have seen the moment of my greatness flicker,
And I have seen the eternal Footman hold my coat, and snicker,
And in short, I was afraid.

And would it have been worth it, after all,
After the cups, the marmalade, the tea,
Among the porcelain, among some talk of you and me,
Would it have been worth while,
To have bitten off the matter with a smile,
To have squeezed the universe into a ball
To roll it towards some overwhelming question,
To say: "I am Lazarus, come from the dead,
Come back to tell you all, I shall tell you all"—
If one, settling a pillow by her head
    Should say: "That is not what I meant at all;
    That is not it, at all."

And would it have been worth it, after all,
Would it have been worth while,
After the sunsets and the dooryards and the sprinkled streets,
After the novels, after the teacups, after the skirts that trail
   along the floor—
And this, and so much more?—
It is impossible to say just what I mean!
But as if a magic lantern threw the nerves in patterns on a screen:
Would it have been worth while
If one, settling a pillow or throwing off a shawl,
And turning toward the window, should say:
    "That is not it at all,
    That is not what I meant, at all."

No! I am not Prince Hamlet, nor was meant to be;
Am an attendant lord, one that will do
To swell a progress, start a scene or two,
Advise the prince; no doubt, an easy tool,
Deferential, glad to be of use,
Politic, cautious, and meticulous;
Full of high sentence, but a bit obtuse;
At times, indeed, almost ridiculous—
Almost, at times, the Fool.

I grow old ... I grow old ...
I shall wear the bottoms of my trousers rolled.

Shall I part my hair behind? Do I dare to eat a peach?
I shall wear white flannel trousers, and walk upon the beach.
I have heard the mermaids singing, each to each.

I do not think that they will sing to me.

I have seen them riding seaward on the waves
Combing the white hair of the waves blown back
When the wind blows the water white and black.

We have lingered in the chambers of the sea
By sea-girls wreathed with seaweed red and brown
Till human voices wake us, and we drown.

Thomas Becket's soliloquy at the end of the first part of *Murder in the Cathedral,* by T.S.Eliot, 1885 – 1965

In the first half of Murder in the Cathedral, *which was written to be performed in the summer of 1935 in Canterbury Cathedral, Archbishop Thomas Becket is visited by four tempters. The first offers him return to the king's favour; the second suggests that he could once again be Chancellor; the third tries to involve him in a coalition against the king; and the fourth provides a picture of the glory of martyrdom, with generations of pilgrims kneeling at his shrine. He rejects them all.*

I first came across this when a teenager, and his soliloquy, which ends the first half of the play, strongly influenced my developing views about the complications of human motivation.

> *Thomas:*
> Now is my way clear, now is the meaning plain:
> Temptation shall not come in this kind again.
> The last temptation is the greatest treason,
> To do the right deed for the wrong reason.
> The natural vigour in the venial sin
> Is the way in which our lives begin.
> Thirty years ago, I sought all the ways
> That lead to pleasure, advancement and praise.
> Delight in sense, in learning and in thought,
> Music and philosophy, curiosity,
> The purple bullfinch in the lilac tree,
> The tiltyard skill, the strategy of chess,
> Love in the garden, singing to the instrument,
> Were all things equally desirable.
> Ambition comes when early force is spent
> And when we find no longer all things possible.
> Ambition comes behind and unobservable.

Sin grows with doing good. When I imposed the King's law
In England, and waged war with him against Toulouse,
I beat the barons at their own game, I
Could then despise the men who thought me most contemptible,
The raw nobility, whose manners matched their finger-nails.
While I ate out of the King's dish
To become servant of God was never my wish.
Servant of God has chance of greater sin
And sorrow, than the man who serves a king.
For those who serve the greater cause may make the
    cause serve them,
Still doing right: and striving with political men
May make that cause political, not by what they do
But by what they are. I know
What yet remains to show you of my history
Will seem to most of you at best futility,
Senseless self-slaughter of a lunatic,
Arrogant passion of a fanatic.
I know that history at all times draws
The strangest consequence from remotest cause.
But for every evil, every sacrilege,
Crime, wrong, oppression and the axe's edge,
Indifference, exploitation, you, and you,
And you, must all be punished. So must you.
I shall no longer act or suffer, to the sword's end.
Now my good Angel, whom God appoints
To be my guardian, hover over the swords' points.

Father and Son: 1939, by William Plomer, 1908 – 1973

A family portrait not too stale to record
Of a pleasant old buffer, nephew to a lord,
Who believed that the bank was mightier than the sword,
And that an umbrella might pacify barbarians abroad:
    Just like an old liberal
    Between the wars.

With an easy existence, and a cosy country place,
And hardly a wrinkle, at sixty, in his face,
Growing old with old books, with old wine, and with
   grace,
Unaware that events move at a breakneck pace:
    Just like an old diehard
    Between the wars.

With innocuous tastes in common with his mate,
A love of his garden and his tidy snug estate,
Of dogs, music and children, and lying in bed late,
And no disposition to quarrel with his fate:
    Just like an old Englishman
    Between the wars.

With no religion or imagination, and a lazy hazy view
Of the great world where trouble kept cropping up anew,
With old clubmen for friends, who would seem stuffy to
   you,
Old faded prigs, but gentlemen (give them their due):
    Just like an old fossil
    Between the wars.

With a kindly old wife who subscribed for the oppressed,
With an OBE and a coiffure like a last year's bird's nest,
Even more tolerant than anyone would have guessed,
Who hoped that in the long run all was for the best:
    Just like an old lady between the wars.

With one child, a son, who in spite of his education
Showed only a modicum of common sense or cultivation,
Sometimes read the *Daily Worker* or the *New Statesman and
    Nation*.
But neither, it must be admitted, with much concentration:
    Just like a young fribble
    Between the wars.

With a firm grasp of half-truths, with political short-sight,
With a belief we could disarm but at the same time fight,
And that only the Left Wing could ever be right,
And that Moscow, of all places, was the sole source of light:
    Just like a young hopeful
    Between the wars.

With a flash flat in Chelsea of a bogus elegance,
With surrealist pictures and books puffed by Gollanz,
With a degree of complacence which nothing could enhance,
And without one sole well-wisher to kick him in the pants:
    Just like a young smarty
    Between the wars.

With a precious mistress who thought she could paint
But could neither show respect nor exercise restraint,
Was a perfect goose-cap, and thought good manners quaint,
With affectation enough to try the patience of a saint:
    Just like a young cutie
    Between the wars.

With a succession of parties for sponges and bores,
With a traffic-jam outside (for they turned up in scores),
With first-rate sherry flowing into second-rate whores,
And third-rate conversation without one single pause:
    Just like a young couple
        Between the wars.

With week-ends in the country and holidays in France,
With promiscuous habits, time to sunbathe and dance,
And even to write books that were hardly worth a glance,
Earning neither reputation nor the publisher's advance:
    Just like a young writer
    Between the wars.

On a Sunday in September there were deck-chairs in the
    sun,
There was argument at lunch between the father and the
    son
(Smoke rose from Warsaw) for the beef was underdone
(Nothing points to heaven now but the anti-aircraft gun):
    With a hey nonny nonny
    And a hi-de-ho.

Oh, the twenties and the thirties were not otherwise
    designed
Than other times when blind men into ditches led the
    blind,
When the rich mouse ate the cheese and the poor mouse
    got the rind,
And man, the self-destroyer, was not lucid in his mind:
    With a hey nonny nonny
    And a hi-de-ho.

Section X

15 Favourites

Fifteen Favourites

1. One sentence from John of Gaunt's dying speech in Act 1 of *Richard II*, by Wiliam Shakespeare, 1564 - 1616   184

2. Fear no more the heat o' th' sun from *Cymbeline*, Act IV, scene ii, by William Shakespeare, 1564 - 1616   185

3. The Daffodils, by William Wordsworth,1770 – 1850   186

4. The Old Familiar Faces, by Charles Lamb, 1775 – 1834   187

5. To Autumn, by John Keats, 1795 – 1821   188

6. I Remember, I Remember, by Thomas Hood, 1799 – 1845   189

7. Break, Break, Break, by Alfred, Lord Tennyson, 1809 – 1892   190

8. Home Thoughts from Abroad, by Robert Browning, 1812 – 1889   191

9. Home Thoughts from the Sea, by Robert Browning, 1812 – 1889   191

10. Requiem, by Robert Louis Stevenson, 1850 – 1894   192

11. Loveliest of Trees, by A.E.Housman, 1859 – 1936   192

12. The Lake Isle of Innisfree, by W.B.Yeats, 1865 – 1939   193

13. The Donkey, by G.K.Chesterton, 1874 – 1936   193

14. Sea Fever, by John Masefield, 1878 – 1967   194

15. Cargoes, by John Masefield, 1878 – 1967   194

One sentence from John of Gaunt's dying speech in
The Tragedy of King Richard the Second,
by William Shakespeare, 1564 – 1616

In this long, quite extraordinary and wonderful sentence the main
verb doesn't arrive until the beginning of the penultimate line.

This royal throne of kings, this scepter'd isle,
This earth of majesty, this seat of Mars,
This other Eden, demi-paradise,
This fortress built by Nature for herself
Against infection and the hand of war,
This happy breed of men, this little world,
This precious stone set in the silver sea,
Which serves it in the office of a wall,
Or as a moat defensive to a house,
Against the envy of less happier lands,
This blessed plot, this earth, this realm, this England,
This nurse, this teeming womb of royal kings,
Fear'd by their breed and famous by their birth,
Renowned for their deeds as far from home,
For Christian service and true chivalry,
As is the sepulchre in stubborn Jewry,
Of the world's ransom, blessed Mary's Son,
This land of such dear souls, this dear dear land,
Dear for her reputation through the world,
Is now leased out, I die pronouncing it,
Like to a tenement or pelting farm.

From Act IV, scene ii of *Cymbeline,*
by Willian Shakespeare, 1564 - 1614

Fear no more the heat o' th' sun,
Nor the furious winter's rages,
Thou thy worldly task hast done,
Home art gone, and ta'en thy wages.
Golden lads and girls all must,
As chimney-sweepers, come to dust.

Fear no more the frown o' th' great;
Thou art past the tyrant's stroke;
Care no more to clothe and eat;
To thee the reed is as the oak:
The sceptre, learning, physic, must
All follow this and come to dust.

Fear no more the lightning-flash
Nor th' all-dreaded thunder-stone.
Fear not slander, censure rash.
Thou hast finish'd joy and moan.
All lovers young, all lovers must
Consign to thee and come to dust.

No exorciser harm thee.
Nor no witchcraft charm thee.
Ghost unlaid forbear thee.
Nothing ill come near thee.
Quiet consummation have,
And renowned be thy grave.

The Daffodils, by William Wordsworth, 1770 – 1850

I wandered lonely as a cloud
That floats on high o'er vales and hills,
When all at once I saw a crowd,
A host of golden daffodils;
Beside the lake, beneath the trees,
Fluttering and dancing in the breeze.

Continuous as the stars that shine
And twinkle on the Milky Way,
They stretched in never-ending line
Along the margin of a bay:
Ten thousand saw I at a glance,
Tossing their heads in sprightly dance.

The waves beside them danced; but they
Out-did the sparkling waves in glee:-
A poet could not but be gay,
In such a jocund company!
I gazed—and gazed—but little thought
What wealth the show to me had brought:

For oft, when on my couch I lie
In vacant or in pensive mood,
They flash upon that inward eye
Which is the bliss of solitude;
And then my heart with pleasure fills
And dances with the daffodils.

The Old Familiar Faces by Charles Lamb, 1775 – 1834

I have had playmates, I have had companions,
In my days of childhood, in my joyful schooldays –
All, all are gone, the old familiar faces.

I have been laughing, I have been carousing,
Drinking late, sitting late, with my bosom cronies –
All, all are gone, the old familiar faces.

I loved a Love once, fairest among women:
Closed are her doors on me, I must not see her –
All, all are gone, the old familiar faces.

I have a friend, a kinder friend has no man:
Like an ingrate, I left my friend abruptly;
Left him, to muse on the old familiar faces.

Ghost-like I paced round the haunts of my childhood,
Earth seem'd a desert I was bound to traverse,
Seeking to find the old familiar faces.

Friend of my bosom, thou more than a brother,
Why wert not thou born in my father's dwelling?
So might we talk of the old familiar faces –

How some they have died, and some they have left me,
And some are taken from me; all are departed –
All, all are gone, the old familiar faces.

To Autumn, by John Keats, 1795 – 1821

Season of mists and mellow fruitfulness,
Close bosom-friend of the maturing sun;
Conspiring with him how to load and bless
With fruit the vines that round the thatch-eves run;
To bend with apples the moss'd cottage-trees,
And fill all fruit with ripeness to the core;
To swell the gourd, and plump the hazel shells
With a sweet kernel; to set budding more,
And still more, later flowers for the bees,
Until they think warm days will never cease,
For Summer has o'er-brimm'd their clammy cells.

Who hath not seen thee oft amid thy store?
Sometimes whoever seeks abroad may find
Thee sitting careless on a granary floor,
Thy hair soft-lifted by the winnowing wind;
Or on a half-reap'd furrow sound asleep,
Drowsed with the fume of poppies, while thy hook
Spares the next swath and all its twinèd flowers:
And sometimes like a gleaner thou dost keep
Steady thy laden head across a brook;
Or by a cider-press, with patient look,
Thou watchest the last oozings hours by hours.

Where are the songs of Spring? Ay, where are they?
Think not of them, thou hast thy music too –
While barrèd clouds bloom the soft-dying day,
And touch the stubble-plains with rosy hue;
Then in a wailful choir the small gnats mourn
Among the river sallows, borne aloft
Or sinking as the light wind lives or dies;
And full-grown lambs loud bleat from hilly bourn;
Hedge-crickets sing; and now with treble soft
The red-breast whistles from a garden-croft;
And gathering swallows twitter in the skies.

I Remember, I Remember, by Thomas Hood, 1789 – 1845

I remember, I remember,
The house where I was born,
The little window where the sun
Came peeping in at morn;
He never came a wink too soon,
Nor brought too long a day,
But now, I often wish the night
Had borne my breath away.

I remember, I remember,
The roses, red and white,
The violets, and the lily-cups,
Those flowers made of light!
The lilacs where the robin built,
And where my brother set
The laburnum on his birthday—
The tree is living yet!

I remember, I remember,
Where I was used to swing,
And thought the air must rush as fresh
To swallows on the wing;
My spirit flew in feathers then,
That is so heavy now,
And summer pools could hardly cool
The fever on my brow!

I remember, I remember,
The fir trees dark and high;
I used to think their slender tops
Were close against the sky:
It was a childish ignorance,
But now 'tis little joy
To know I'm farther off from heav'n
Than when I was a boy.

Break, Break, Break, by Alfred, Lord Tennyson, 1809 – 1892

This was the very first poem I ever learnt. No-one asked me to. Indeed, no-one ever asked me to learn any poems, and I cannot remember just what age I was when I learnt this. I simply loved the pictures in words of the ships and the stones at the edge of the sea, and the fisherman's boy with his sister and the sailor lad singing, and I felt its sadness. I must have known it for about forty years when my first wife died at the age of forty-seven. It was only then that I felt its power in a manner never felt before.

> Break, break, break,
>   On thy cold gray stones, O Sea!
> And I would that my tongue could utter
>   The thoughts that arise in me.
>
> O, well for the fisherman's boy,
>   That he shouts with his sister at play!
> O, well for the sailor lad,
>   That he sings in his boat on the bay!
>
> And the stately ships go on
>   To their haven under the hill;
> But O for the touch of a vanish'd hand,
>   And the sound of a voice that is still!
>
> Break, break, break
>   At the foot of thy crags, O Sea!
> But the tender grace of a day that is dead
>   Will never come back to me.

Home Thoughts from Abroad,
by Robert Browning, 1812 – 1889

Oh, to be in England
Now that April's there,
And whoever wakes in England
Sees, some morning, unaware,
That the lowest boughs and the brushwood sheaf
Round the elm-tree bole are in tiny leaf,
While the chaffinch sings on the orchard bough
In England—now!

And after April, when May follows,
And the whitethroat builds, and all the swallows!
Hark, where my blossomed pear-tree in the hedge
Leans to the field and scatters on the clover
Blossoms and dewdrops—at the bent spray's edge—
That's the wise thrush; he sings each song twice over,
Lest you should think he never could recapture
The first fine careless rapture!
And though the fields look rough with hoary dew,
All will be gay when noontide wakes anew
The buttercups, the little children's dower—
Far brighter than this gaudy melon-flower!

Home thoughts from the Sea, also by Robert Browning

Nobly, nobly Cape Saint Vincent to the North-west died away;
Sunset ran, one glorious blood-red, reeking into Cadiz Bay;
Bluish 'mid the burning water, full in face Trafalgar lay;
In the dimmest North-east distance dawned Gibraltar grand
    and grey;
"Here and here did England help me: how can I help
    England?" - say,
Whoso turns as I, this evening, turn to God to praise and pray,
While Jove's planet rises yonder, silent over Africa.

Loveliest of Trees, by A.E.Housman, 1859 – 1936

Loveliest of trees, the cherry now
Is hung with bloom along the bough,
And stands about the woodland ride
Wearing white for Eastertide.

Now, of my three-score years and ten,
Twenty will not come again,
And take from seventy years a score,
It only leaves me fifty more.

And since for seeing things in bloom
Fifty years is little room,
About the woodland I will go
To see the cherry hung with snow.

The Lake Isle of Innisfree, by W.B.Yeats, 1865 – 1939

I will arise and go now, and go to Innisfree,
And a small cabin build there, of clay and wattles made;
Nine bean-rows will I have there, a hive for the honey-bee,
And live alone in the bee-loud glade.

And I shall have some peace there, for peace comes dropping
    slow,
Dropping from the veils of the morning to where the cricket
    sings;
There midnight's all a glimmer, and noon a purple glow,
And evening full of the linnet's wings.

I will arise and go now, for always night and day
I hear lake water lapping with low sounds by the shore;
While I stand on the roadway, or on the pavements grey,
I hear it in the deep heart's core.

Requiem, by Robert Louis Stevenson, 1850 – 1894

Under the wide and starry sky
Dig the grave and let me lie.
Glad did I live and gladly die,
And I laid me down with a will.

This be the verse you grave for me:
"Here he lies where he longed to be,
Home is the sailor, home from sea,
And the hunter home from the hill."

The Donkey, by G.K.Chesterton, 1874 – 1936

When fishes flew and forests walked
  And figs grew upon thorn,
Some moment when the moon was blood
  Then surely I was born.

With monstrous head and sickening cry
  And ears like errant wings,
The devil's walking parody
  Of all four-footed things.

The tattered outlaw of the earth,
  Of ancient crooked will;
Starve, scourge, deride me: I am dumb,
  I keep my secret still.

Fools! For I also had my hour;
  One far fierce hour and sweet:
There was a shout about my ears,
  And palms before my feet.

Sea Fever, by John Masefield, 1878 – 1967

I must go down to the seas again, to the lonely sea and the sky,
And all I ask is a tall ship and a star to steer her by,
And the wheel's kick and the wind's song and the white sail's
   shaking,
And a grey mist on the sea's face, and a grey dawn breaking.

I must go down to the seas again, for the call of the running tide
Is a wild call and a clear call that may not be denied;
And all I ask is a windy day with the white clouds flying,
And the flung spray and the blown spume, and the sea-gulls crying.

I must go down to the seas again, to the vagrant gypsy life,
To the gull's way and the whale's way where the wind's like a
   whetted knife;
And all I ask is a merry yarn from a laughing fellow-rover,
And quiet sleep and a sweet dream when the long trick's over.

Cargoes, by John Masefield, 1878 – 1967

Quinquireme of Nineveh from distant Ophir
Rowing home to haven in sunny Palestine,
With a cargo of ivory,
And apes and peacocks,
Sandalwood, cedarwood, and sweet white wine.

Stately Spanish galleon coming from the Isthmus,
Dipping through the Tropics by the palm-green shores,
With a cargo of diamonds,
Emeralds, amethysts,
Topazes, and cinnamon and gold moidores.

Dirty British coaster with a salt-caked smoke stack
Butting through the Channel in the mad March days,
With a cargo of Tyne coal,
Road-rail, pig-lead,
Firewood, iron-ware, and cheap tin trays.

Index of opening words

Page

Abou ben Adhem (may his tribe increase)   90
A chieftain to the highlands bound   88
'A cold coming we had of it'   124
A family portrait not too stale to record   179
All abbesses deserve to die   3
All the world's a stage, and all the men and women   155
And did those feet in ancient time   136
A soldier passed me in the freshly fallen snow   67
A sudden blow. The great wings beating still   14
As we get older we do not get any younger   78
Avenge, O Lord, thy slaughtered saints   11

Bent double like old beggars under sacks   66
Blessed is the man that hath not walked in the counsel   21
Bloody men are like bloody buses   83
Break, break, break on thy cold gray stones, O sea   190
By the waters of Babylon we sat down and wept   30

Cut down that timber! Bells, too many and strong   16

Dear Lord and Father of mankind   137
1. Don't see him. Don't phone or write a letter.   5
Drake he's in his hammock an' a thousand miles away   62

Earth hath not anything to show more fair   12
Everyone suddenly burst out singing   64

Page

Fear no more the heat o' th' sun   185

Gather ye rosebuds while ye may   36
Give rest, O Christ, to thy servant with thy saints   132
God be in my head and in my understanding   132
God is our hope and strength   25
Go, lovely Rose! Tell her that wastes her time, and me   37
'Good-morning, good-morning' the General said   64

Had we but world enough and time   39
Half a league, half a league, half a league onwards   60
Here lies a great and mighty king   74
How beautiful are thy feet with shoes, O prince's daughter!   34
How do I love thee, let me count the ways   44

I, being born a woman and distressed   15
I danced in the morning when the earth was begun   145
I eat my peas with honey   74
If I should die, think only this of me   65
If I should learn in some quite casual way   15
If you can keep your head when all about you are
    losing theirs   167
I have had playmates, I have had companions   187
I hope I can trust you, friends, not to use our relationship   85
I met a traveller from an antique land   12
Immortal, invisible, God only wise   140
I must go down to the seas again,   194
In the bleak midwinter frosty wind made moan   141
In Xanadu did Kubla Khan a stately pleasure dome decree   158
I remember, I remember the house where I was born   189
"Is there anybody there?" said the Traveller   115
I think I am in love with A.E.Housman   5
It was on a Friday morning when they took me from my cell   146

Page

I vow to thee, my country, all earthly things above   143
I wandered lonely as a cloud that floats on high   186
I will arise and go now, and go to Innisfree   192
I will lift up mine eyes unto the hills   28

Jenny kissed me when we met,   4
John Anderson, my Jo, John   41

Lars Porsena of Clusium, by the nine gods he swore   91/92
Legate, I heard the news last night, my cohort ordered
   home   168
Let me not to the marriage of true minds admit
   impediment   10
Let us go then, you and I, when the evening is spread out   172
'Let us not speak, for the love we have for one another'   50
Lord, now lettest Thou Thy servant depart in peace   20
Lord, who shall dwell in thy tabernacle   23
Love bade me welcome: yet my soul drew back   35
Loveliest of trees, the cherry now   192

Most near, most dear, most loved and most far   16
Much have I travelled in the realms of gold   13
My candle burns at both ends   5
My heart aches, and a drowsy numbness pains my sense   162
My heart has made its mind up   84
My heart leaps up when I behold a rainbow in the sky   4
My love in her attire doth show her wit   3
My soul doth magnify the Lord   20

Nobly, nobly Cape St Vincent to the North-west
   died away   191
No-one so much as you loves this my clay   48
Not a drum was heard, not a funeral note   58
Now is my way clear, now is the meaning plain   177
Now on this out of season afternoon   127

Page

O be joyful in the Lord all ye lands   28
O come, let us sing unto the Lord   27
O for a Muse of fire that would ascend the brightest
    heaven   150
O how amiable are thy dwellings   26
O Lord our Governor, how excellent is thy name   22
Once more unto the breach, dear friends, once more   152
On Waterloo Bridge, where we said our good-byes,   84
O praise God in his holiness, praise Him in the firmament   31
O to be in England now that April's there   191
Out of the deep have I called unto thee   29
O what can ail thee, knight at arms   42
O world invisible we view thee   144

Phone for the fish knives, Norman   82

Quinquireme of Nineveh, from distant Ophir   194

Remember me when I am gone away   13
Robert of Sicily, brother of Pope Urbane   99

Say not the struggle nought availeth   139
Season of mists and mellow fruitfulness   188
Sexual intercourse began in nineteen sixty-three   79
Shall I compare thee to a summer's day?   16
She died in an upstairs bedroom   128
Since there's no help, come, let us kiss and part   9
So Abram rose, and clave the wood, and went   126
Some men never think of it. You did.   83
Stop all the clocks, cut off the telephone   50

Page

Teach me, my God and King, in all things Thee to see 133
Tell me not, sweet, I am unkinde 57
That's my last duchess painted on the wall 165
That which her slender waist confin'd 38
The beauty of Israel is slain upon thy high places 56
The Chief Defect of Henry King was chewing
    little bits of String 114
The Lord is my shepherd: therefore can I lack nothing 24
The Lord's my shepherd, I'll not want 134
The noble horse with courage in his eye 70
The owl and the pussycat went to sea 75
The rain set early in tonight 106
There is a green hill far away 138
There's a famous seaside place called Blackpool 121
There was a young curate of Crediton 6
There was a young curate of Kew 6
There was a young poet called Spends 6
There was an old man of Japan 6
The sun was shining on the sea 108
The things about you I appreciate may seem indelicate 51
The wind was a torrent of darkness among the gusty trees 117
They fuck you up, your Mum and Dad 80
They told me, Heraclitus, they told me you were dead 44
This royal throne of kings, this sceptered isle 184
Thou still unravished bride of quietness 160
Three summers since I chose a maid 112
Three weeks gone and the combatants gone 71
Today we have naming of parts 69
To the man-in-the-street, who, I'm sorry to say 5
Twas brillig and the slithy toves 76

Under the wide and starry sky dig the grave and let me lie 193

Page

Wee, sleekit, cow'rin', tim'rous beastie — 156
We praise Thee, O Lord — 19
Western Wind, when will thou blow? — 3
What lips my lips have kissed and where and why — 14
What passing bells for these who die like cattle — 65
What's he that wishes so? My cousin Westmorland? — 153
Whenas in silks my Julia goes — 4
When fishes flew and forests walked — 193
When I am an old woman I shall wear purple — 81
When I am living in the Midlands — 170
When I am sad and weary — 5
When I consider how my light is spent — 11
Where the thistle lifts a purple crown six feet out of the turf — 45
Who would true valour see — 135

Yes, I remember Adlestrop, the name — 63
'You are old, Father William', the young man said — 77

Lightning Source UK Ltd.
Milton Keynes UK
UKHW011957130222
398631UK00001B/17